Media Professionalism and Training

Key Concerns in Media Studies

Series Editor: **Andrew Crisell**

Within the context of today's global, digital environment, *Key Concerns in Media Studies* addresses themes and concepts that are integral to the study of media. Concisely written by leading academics, the books consider the historical development of these themes and the theories that underpin them and assess their overall significance, using up-to-date examples and case studies throughout. By giving a clear overview of each topic, the series provides an ideal starting point for all students of modern media.

Published

Paul Bowman   *Culture and the Media*

Andrew Crisell   *Liveness and Recording in the Media*

Tim Dwyer   *Legal and Ethical Issues in the Media*

Gerard Goggin   *New Technologies and the Media*

Shaun Moores   *Media, Place and Mobility*

Forthcoming

Bob Franklin   *Politics, News and the Media*

Gerard Goggin and Kathleen Ellis   *Disability and the Media*

David Hendy   *Public Service Broadcasting*

Niall Richardson and Sadie Wearing   *Gender and the Media*

Media Professionalism and Training

Sarah Niblock

School of Arts, Brunel University, UK

palgrave
macmillan

First published 2013 by
PALGRAVE MACMILLAN

Palgrave Macmillan in the UK is an imprint of Macmillan Publishers Limited, registered in England, company number 785998, of Houndmills, Basingstoke, Hampshire RG21 6XS.

Palgrave Macmillan in the US is a division of St Martin's Press LLC, 175 Fifth Avenue, New York, NY 10010.

Palgrave Macmillan is the global academic imprint of the above companies and has companies and representatives throughout the world.

Palgrave® and Macmillan® are registered trademarks in the United States, the United Kingdom, Europe and other countries.

ISBN 978–0–230–29282–6

This book is printed on paper suitable for recycling and made from fully managed and sustained forest sources. Logging, pulping and manufacturing processes are expected to conform to the environmental regulations of the country of origin.

A catalogue record for this book is available from the British Library.

A catalog record for this book is available from the Library of Congress.

Printed in China

Contents

Preface

In an age when anyone with a broadband connection and a mobile phone can call themselves a media practitioner, uploading content to the Internet without a modicum of training or experience, the question of professionalism has never been more acute. In 2005, the chair of the National Union of Journalists' professional training committee Chris Wheal described journalism as 'an unregulated job title that is open to charlatans, miscreants and the literary equivalent of snake-oil salesmen. It is no wonder our work is held in such low public esteem' (Wheal, 2005). Now anyone and everyone can be a reporter, commentator, editor or video maker, whether or not they get paid for it. Or can they?

When I started writing this book, the mainstream media – the so-called Fourth Estate – were and still are engulfed by a torrent of criticism, analysis and reorganization, mired in doubt and controversy over standards, ethics and practices. News International and, a few months later, the BBC became embroiled in criticism about a lack of journalistic standards over, respectively, the hacking of mobile-phone messages and the decision to drop a *Newsnight* investigation into alleged sexual abuse by former BBC presenter Jimmy Savile. Now the Leveson Report has been published, and media owners are debating its implications, some claim its tenets have had a 'chilling effect' already on reporting, even before a new press regulatory body is agreed and formed.

Against this backdrop of editorial trepidation, countless long-standing media brands are closing or recalibrating to counter the effects of advertising revenue downturns and poor outcomes for corporate shareholders. Given the vast numbers of people employed in the journalism industry globally, and the many tens of thousands wanting to break in to the media every year, it is urgent that we re-evaluate the role of the media professional and the routes by which new entrants achieve this position.

This book, based on extensive interviews and research at some of the most famous editorial brands, offers timely insights into what skills and qualities new entrants really need if they are to succeed in this new digital, global media landscape. The most dazzling proficiency with online technology means little without the mindset to put those skills into ethical, journalistic use. Advanced academic and vocational qualifications are also not necessarily a predictor of a person's aptitude in the newsroom. The journalists of tomorrow need to be clever, canny operators to achieve success – and the opportunities are there for the best.

So what has changed and why is the book necessary? In a nutshell, new media technology is only in its earliest infancy yet it has already wrought significant changes in the relationship between journalists and their audiences. Some observers have called this the age of the media 'produser' as the producers and users of media messages merge into one. The old 'top-down' models of communication, where the elite editors told the rest of us what they thought we should know, are redundant. The journalists of today and tomorrow need a far more nuanced understanding of communication techniques and audience psychology even before they get onto the fundamentals of writing and reporting. So these are different times and we are only at the beginning of the journey. Whether you see this new 'Fifth Estate' of digitally active citizens as a threat or an opportunity, one thing is certain: the media world is crying out for leaders to take it forward. In the current climate of uncertainty, skills are become less important than mindset and leadership, and that is what this book aims to impart.

To put this transformation into some context, let us start by briefly clarifying the distinctions between the Fourth and Fifth Estates. The Fourth Estate generally refers to photographers, journalists, television broadcasters and radio announcers, among others. Statesman and philosopher Edmund Burke is believed to have coined the term in 1787 when the House of Commons first opened up to press reporting. Many people generally agree that the Fourth Estate has immense political and social power, thanks to the fact that the Press can be used to shape societies while imparting news of note and commentary of interest. Because the Fourth Estate is recognized as such an important body, many nations have laws which protect the rights of the Press, ensuring that citizens have access to reporting on matters of interest and of note. The origins of the terms are best explained within the context of the medieval 'estates of the realm'. In medieval society, three 'estates' were formally recognized: the clergy, the nobility and the commoners. Each estate had a very distinct social role and a certain level of power, and the idea of the estates of the realm became so entrenched in European society that it still lives on, to some extent, although society is far more egalitarian today.[1]

From bloggers to citizen journalists, to campaigners, to networks of investigative researchers, there is a growing Fifth Estate of activity working alongside the Fourth Estate or in opposition to the mainstream. Academic authors such as Stephen D. Cooper (2006) describe how the Internet has enabled networked citizens to hold the other estates accountable, including the Fourth. So in a day and age when the means to self-mediate have never been more widespread, what does it mean to be a media 'professional', someone who is paid to do the job of bringing news, features and other information to us in its myriad forms and platforms?

This is a long-standing debate, even within traditional journalism. As one of the most commonly vilified occupations, its practitioners have for a long time clamoured for status while at the same time identifying with the grass roots notion of a skilled tradesperson. There has been a raft of articles, books, lectures and theses about the status of the media, the opportunities and challenges to standards that professionalism suggests. When I started writing this book, I did so in response to the numerous passionate defences of the industry by high-profile members of its workforce in the face of perceived threats to the public interest from untrained amateurs with a home hub. However, in the space of a few months, the critics have become as fearful about the threat to professional mores from those actually within the occupation, not just outside. Revelations about the extent of illegal behaviour by journalists working for newspapers in the United Kingdom have cast doubt on the prevailing dichotomy that professional equals good and amateur equals bad.

There even seems to have been something of a volte-face about Internet-generated sources of information. If evidence for this upturn were needed, it can be found in the zeal with which prestigious news organizations worldwide have embraced and analysed secret, leaked official documents disseminated by websites such as *WikiLeaks*.

But there remains one resonant undercurrent in each response. Mainstream news organizations have used both instances – at opposite ends of the 'ethical' scale – to vigorously defend the need for professional journalism, either to defend against 'unprofessional' behaviour or to undertake painstaking analysis of data. Likewise, media activists, citizen journalists and campaigners also call for heightened professionalism to foster new creative ways of working in the public interest. This book will examine closely what media professionalism means in this context and whether it can be learnt or acquired. Whatever different stakeholders may feel about the definition of media working, there can be no dispute that journalism in the West, and increasingly in the developing world, has adopted more and more of the characteristics of a profession. This process has accelerated over the past 30 years with the growth in global media and the relative decline in nationally and locally owned companies.

This book goes beyond merely rehearsing the various theories and theses on whether journalism can be defined as a trade, a craft, a profession or, recently, a semi-profession. I shall cover those definitions through the perspectives and words of several influential commentators. However, this book will delve deeper into the concepts and standpoints that seem to be taken as read in media criticism and commentary, yet should still be openly contested. The terms 'professional' and 'professionalism' are in themselves ideologically loaded, which means their definitions are as dynamic and culturally specific as the industry in question.

Given the many viewpoints both within and without the industry, this book will interrogate the following questions in order to evaluate the current state of journalism training and education and evaluate its efficacy for preparing the next generation of editorial leaders.

- How has the social role and status of journalism evolved?
- What training and education routes are there into journalism and are they fit for purpose?
- Once in, how do journalists learn the ropes and advance their careers?
- Has the drive for professionalism worked to raise standards, given the crises on both sides of the Atlantic?
- Is citizen journalism a threat or an opportunity to drive up standards and make journalism more professional?
- What does the successful twenty-first-century media professional look like, and can anyone acquire those attributes?

Introduction

Examining media training and professionalism reflexively

Studies of news over the past 30 years or so have made us accustomed to thinking of journalism as a part of a process of manufacture (Cohen and Young, 1981; Tuchman, 2003; Schudson, 2005), but those processes involve very human judgements and subjectivities. New entrants and trainees must learn how to report, write and package 'professionally' to meet production demands, so that they are deemed worthy of the title 'journalist' and can advance their careers. Ericson et al. (1989) showed how the journalists in their study learned a 'vocabulary of precedents', accumulating a stock of knowledge from which to draw. This study returns to a similar research approach to help us to better understand this process and learn, with reference to the wider occupational community and in changing working conditions and employment contexts, how ordinary journalists develop an understanding of what 'journalism' means. In other words, how do journalists learn to 'do journalism' in a form that is acceptable to employers and colleagues?

The critical approach of this book will be reflexive, as the best way of examining media professionalism and training is to examine it at very close range and speak to its practitioners. Sandelowski and Barroso (2002, p. 222) explain what reflexivity means in an academic context:

> Reflexivity is a hallmark of excellent qualitative research, and it entails the ability and willingness of researchers to acknowledge and take account of the many ways they themselves influence research findings and thus what comes to be accepted as knowledge. Reflexivity implies the ability to reflect inward towards oneself as an inquirer; outward to the cultural, historical, linguistic, political and other forces that shape everything about inquiry; and, in between researcher and participant to the social interaction they share.

Nightingale and Cromby (1999, p. 228) have further divided reflexivity into a number of subcategories to helpfully illustrate potential approaches in a multidisciplinary context. For instance, epistemological reflexivity requires the researcher

> to engage with questions such as: How has the research question defined and limited what can be 'found?' Thus, epistemological reflexivity encourages us to reflect upon the assumptions (about the world, about knowledge) that we have made in the course of the research, and it helps us to think about the implications of such assumptions for the research and its findings. How has the design of the study and the method of analysis 'constructed' the data and the findings? How could the research question have been investigated differently? To what extent would this have given rise to a different understanding of the phenomenon under investigation?

This critical stance gives way to understanding, theory and changing the very assumptions that may have been hidden before any reflexive action are at issue.

As a journalist, educator and researcher, I am aware of, and fascinated by, the comparative and often conflicting pressures that each occupational identity brings to the task of untangling the various themes and debates of this book. Therefore, I attempt to reflect a broad range of perspectives in my analysis and thereby articulate media production as a process not just in terms of its demonstrable, visible output. I also seek to contextualize media professionalism and training socio-historically and socioculturally for transparency. But rather than essentially looking back over the developments of an industry and its practices, this book will be looking ahead to the future of media professionalism and training. The underlying narrative will be to see what its complex trajectory might illuminate and indicate about the path ahead.

The first chapter will introduce the reader to the key themes and terms of the book, providing a critical account of how the media originated as trades and have now become professionalized. It will look at how a trade might be differentiated from a profession in the context of the media, before closely examining the key facets that give the media a professional inflection. It is possible to trace how the professionalization of the media has gone hand in hand with technological advances and a shift from local to global models of ownership. In journalism, technology has enabled the systematization and routinization of newsroom functions. An example would be the invention of the trans-Atlantic cable; commonplace techniques, such as the inverted triangle news structure, were born out of the demand for consistency, speed and brevity. A further example is the rise of the big global news agencies, owned by companies with direct ties to the banking industry and situated in or close to the stock exchanges of London, Paris and Berlin. The chapter will then explore how the media world continues to evolve towards an ever more professionalized state. Simultaneously, the chapter will outline efforts to diversify a professional model of the media, specifically the rise of user-generated content. The chapter will close by considering critical questions arising from the shift from trade to profession. Should the media's role be to deliver audiences to advertisers – or should they be serving the communities they cover? The first step to unpacking this is to explore how media professionals are recruited and trained.

Reports and studies over the past few years have questioned the recruitment strategies of media companies and the institutions that prepare them for the workplace. The chapter will begin by outlining some of the concerns before describing how media training has evolved from trade to profession over the last few decades. It will use the case study of the history of the National Council of the Training of Journalists in the United Kingdom, and how new entrants aged 16 were once trained and indentured. We have now moved to a situation in the United States, Europe, Australia and in the growing economies of Asia, of graduates self-funding their training and entering with Master's-level qualifications. Given this global shift, the chapter will critically evaluate the current aims and scope of the content of media training, and who shapes it. A crucial question will be who should provide and fund that training, given the concerns raised about the admission policies of certain universities. Does an academic training adequately prepare students and provide sufficient access for a diverse range of entrants? Issues around inclusivity in the media will be key to this chapter, as will questions around the funding and future of training.

Once recruits have entered the media, how are they socialized to perform the role of a fully-fledged professional practitioner? Chapter 3 will ask this very important question. Few ordinary members of the public witness how media forms are produced and how their producers interact with one another. At one time, media practitioners learnt their trade through immersion and close mentoring by more senior colleagues. There were set career-progression paths and firm job divisions and hierarchies. Today, the media workplace is characterized by multitasking with new entrants often teaching established staff new skills. The chapter will explore how new employees negotiate the unfamiliar territory of the workplace. It will identify and evaluate the mechanisms used by media organizations to assert control, to monitor performance and maintain leadership. It will illuminate whether employees have any power to resist or challenge decisions made by their colleagues or superiors or whether they must simply conform. The chapter will conclude by exploring the idea of the competitor-colleague, and what their relationship is with others in their field. Competition between media organizations now seems to exist within and between close colleagues, as they fight to maintain their short-term rolling contracts or freelancing commissions.

Chapter 4 will examine to whom the media professional is, or should be, accountable. Throughout history, the media have fought vigorously to protect their autonomy and freedom from overarching state control. While subject to some state and self-regulation, the media are for the most part independent. What is the position for the professionalized media with regard to media ethics, regulation and the law? Should the media's independence be protected from interference if it is to function as a watchdog? It will explore how the professionalization of the media to support the global business imperative of media companies may in fact be as much or even more of a threat to media freedom than state oversight.

The professional model of media is clearly now under threat, given the decline in advertising revenue, subscriptions and the growth in free media forms. Chapter 5 will critically evaluate the impact of user-generated content, online television, citizen journalism, networked journalism along with blogging and other social-networking formats. Are these new formats indicative of an emerging backlash against the Fourth Estate? Perhaps non-professional media, or an alliance between paid and unpaid practitioners may be even better placed to serve the public interest.

As well as providing a critical summary of the preceding chapters, the Conclusion will consider what a media professional's identity and function should be in the digital age.

This book also seeks to negotiate an accommodation between two quite different yet increasingly interlinked institutions – journalism and education. As a practitioner-academic, I have to take a conceptual and reflexive overview of the situation. This is firmly underlined by a compulsion to educate and research within a constantly shifting environment. The fault lines between education and training and the journalism industry are all too often viewed as indicative of discord. The Fifth Estate demonstrates clearly how we need to start to detach journalism from capital, to view journalism as transcending media forms and institutions and to strip it back from brokerage to its fundamental and abiding purpose – the capture and relay of information of interest and import by and between individuals and groups. In that way, when the pieces start to fall towards earth we start to see the factors and forces at play in sculpting journalism and its people, which includes by extension its users. There are endless conferences and debates about where journalism is going and what its future might look like. This is not one of those; it is about seeking to expose the facets that have gone into professionalism of one aspect of journalism – the mainstream media industry which is by no means its totality – so that we might be able to reflect, as practitioners, educators, trainers and consumers, on its significant potential if we decouple it for a moment from its defining institutions and approaches.

1 From 'Trade' to 'Profession'

Andrew Keen, author of *The Cult of the Amateur* (2007), argues that media messages produced and distributed for free by non-professionals undermine the authority and purpose of traditional outlets such as newspapers, magazines, broadcasting, music and films. Against this confused backdrop, it is understandably hard for anyone thinking of a media career to know what lies ahead. But what is evident is that the industry and society are keenly debating what the attributes of 'professionalism' are and trying to draw clear boundaries as well as to cultivate strong leaders.

The term 'professional' has become synonymous with journalists who are paid for their services. The word is often used to distinguish between journalists who are employed by a media organization as opposed to independent bloggers and citizen journalists who might loosely be termed the 'Fifth Estate'. Reporters, feature writers and editors are proud to declare themselves to be part of a profession. As the boundaries of professional identity and trade allegiance are being fiercely defended against the rapid rise of the Fifth Estate at the start of the new millennium, there is even more introspection as to how journalism would define and protect its occupational status. But what does journalism as a profession constitute? And can it neatly be defined thus?

The journey towards the professionalization of journalism began in earnest in the nineteenth century; yet, debate still rages more than 100 years later over it's occupational status. Some maintain that it is a trade with its roots in the local community, delivering a service or commodity to its clientele. Others increasingly view journalism as possessing a higher moral imperative of public interest divorced from its commercial aim, as evidenced by its associated codes of practice. In this way, it has much in common with established professions such as law or medicine. Key signs of this include the emergence of a professional journalistic ideology (such as attention to objectivity), the growth of professional institutions and graduate-level qualifications. It has also been noted that journalistic professional values are becoming increasingly universal as the media become more global and corporatized; how journalists view ethics, standards and priorities are fairly universal despite some cultural and historical nuances (Weaver, 2005).

There have been several 'professional moments' during journalism's development. By examining how professionalism has been manifested over time, we can see that journalism is actually a very dynamic occupation that adapts according to its context. The picture that emerges is that journalism's adoption of professional mores is only partial and is indeed superficial, aimed primarily at sustaining the profit-motive. Perhaps a new set of values is needed to take its place and restore public faith.

Journalism as a trade or craft

The BBC political editor Andrew Marr described journalism as 'my trade' in his 2004 brief history of the Press, *My Trade*. It is easy to see how journalists might identify with trades- and craftspeople. A tradesperson is a skilled manual worker whose status, economically and socially, is considered somewhere between a labourer and a professional. Examples of tradespeople might be welders or electricians. The practitioners possess a high degree of both practical and theoretical knowledge of their trade. Traditionally, a tradesperson needs to be permanently involved in the exchange of goods or services to make ends meet. It is certainly an area we will examine much more closely in the context of the media. It is interesting to consider how much the profit-motive in commercial media production impacts on the determination of journalism in particular as a trade or profession. This question will be examined in more detail later in this chapter.

A craft lies somewhere between an *art* (which relies on talent) and a *science* (which relies on knowledge). The English word *craft* is roughly equivalent to the ancient Greek term *techne*, meaning skill or art. It tends to be most often associated with the decorative arts such as pottery, tapestry or certain types of woodwork. Typically, a trades- or craftsperson would serve an apprenticeship, learning on the job under the close tutelage of a senior practitioner. Once qualified, they would search for a place to set up their own business and make their own living.

This corresponds with journalism; newspapers especially were once locally owned and recruited staff from their catchment areas based on their expert local knowledge and contacts. Editorial staff would start their careers as 'copy boys' and, less frequently, girls, running errands for the editor as they gradually learnt how to report and write. Only after several years' experience would a reporter have the opportunity to train in editorial production and become a sub-editor.

This step-by-step approach to mastery of a skill, which involves obtaining a certain amount of training through observation and experience, still survives in some countries. However, crafts even more than trades have undergone deep structural changes since the Industrial Revolution during which time the mass production of goods limited crafts to areas of life that industry could not satisfy, either due to its modes of functioning or because mass-produced goods would not meet the preferences of potential buyers. The fact that so many journalists are keen, especially at the current time of digital mediation, to identify with the model of trades- or craftsperson is a reaction to the increasing mechanization and mass production of journalism, in which the editorial staff are cogs in a very big wheel. Journalists may be very keen to protect the perceived 'artisan' expert status of their field. A trades- or craftsperson also suggests that an individual's working varies closely with their clientele, rather than in the distanced manner an industry might suggest. It also connotes an element of individual artistry and autonomy rather than an individual beholden to set processes and practices.

But there are some limits to classifying journalism as a trade or craft. It could be reasonably argued that journalism requires more than being part of a news production line if it is to move forward. Journalists are certainly required to gather and re-present information but, like doctors who possess accumulated knowledge and experience, they use their seasoned judgement to make editorial decisions. Technological changes have removed some of journalism's trade and craft elements such as being physically out and about in a community. It still takes craft to write the story but the art of finding the story is diminishing with research suggesting that 90 per cent of stories are generated by press releases (Lewis et al., 2008). But the media industry has the same economic structures and developments as any other commodity-based sector. It is a labour product with its end result the commodity of news, which is then marketed, sold and consumed.

Defining professions

The term 'profession' has many meanings and is used in a variety of contexts. *The Oxford English Dictionary* (*OED*) (1997, p. 572) states:

> The occupation which one professes to be skilled in and to follow. A vocation which a professed knowledge of some department of

learning or science is used in its application to the affairs of others or in an art upon it. Applied Spec. to the three learned professions of divinity, law and medicine, also to the military professions.

(OED, Vol. XII)

The three 'learned' professions of divinity, law and medicine are specifically mentioned. Therefore, a fundamental question would be: why were these occupations singled out and labelled professions? This is an important issue because defining professions by reference to the traits of these three old occupations helps draw a boundary around the concept and, consequently, excludes other practices that do not display these characteristics.[1]

Journalism presents a challenge to formal notions of professions such as medicine or law due to its diverse and undefined nature. Jeremy Tunstall has described journalism as vague and hard to define as opposed to law and medicine that are more sharply bordered or neatly defined. He described the term 'journalism' as a 'label which people engaged in a very diverse range of activities apply to themselves' (Tunstall, 1973, p. 98). Writing 40 years ago, Tunstall could not envision journalism gaining the professional status of, say, law or medicine. This suggests that the 'professional' status of journalism might have been applied as a defence mechanism or a means to convey the image of respectability rather than as an accurate representation of the diversity of its practices. Characterizing the professions has also long posed a challenge to social scientists. None of the founding fathers of sociology – Marx, Weber and Durkheim – paid much attention to the status of professions in their respective theories of the divisions in society (Tumber and Prentoulis in de Burgh, 2005, p. 58).

The twentieth century was defined by economic growth and increased social mobility as the United Kingdom moved towards a post-industrial society (Bell, 1973). Bell argued that the older industrial manual occupations would give way to a post-industrial, knowledge-based society, where technical and professional white-collar workers would form the major productive base. Recent sociological studies appear to support Bell's claim and demonstrate sustained growth in the importance of the 'professional classes'. For example, Heath and Payne (2000) completed a study of social mobility, which built on the methodologies employed by sociologists in earlier seminal works, such as Goldthorpe (1980).

There are two typical scholarly approaches to professionalism that can help us to understand media professionalism. One approach is to examine how certain occupations accumulate professional traits that distinguish them from non-professional roles. Another approach takes a more socio-historical route to chart how the development of professions is related to broader contextual changes over time. Both approaches have their strengths and weaknesses when applied to journalism.

Studying the traits associated with professionalism was particularly popular among sociologists in the 1960s and 1970s. Millerson (1964) summarized the characteristics of a profession:

> Knowledge monopoly: no-one outside the profession has the knowledge and ability to do the work of the profession;

> Exclusivity: a clear division of labour, and the power to exclude outsiders (e.g., by enforcing some kind of legitimisation);

> Professional bodies: strong professional organisations with ethical rules and standards and internal systems dealing with those breaking the ethical rules of the profession;

> Education and training: strong professional education and research. A long academic education is associated with a profession;

> Codes: an ideology that advocates greater commitment to doing good work than to economic gain and to quality rather than the economic efficiency of work.
>
> (Cited in Nygren, 2011, p. 208)

A limitation of this approach when applied to journalism is that ideal traits can change over time and are dependent on dynamic contexts. This has been particularly evident in the move to graduate intake rather than school leavers in the past 30 years. A further issue is that fixed-trait models suggest an industry-led approach. They do not account for the actions taken by occupational groups in the media to ensure they are *seen* as professional and thus elevate their own status. This suggests a departure from traits towards a power-based model. To constitute a profession, members of an occupation have to be able to control their own work and to have autonomy in their everyday practice. Sociologists suggest a number of means by which professionals can exercise this control (Selander, 1989; Friedson, 2001).

Reflecting on the work of Millerson (1964), Johnson (1972) states that the dynamic process of professionalization as a concept can be seen as a 'straight jacket imposing a view of occupational development which is uniform between cultures and uni-linear in character' (Johnson, 1972,

p. 37). Johnson then proceeds to develop a definition firmly viewed from his own critical perspective: 'Professionalism becomes redefined as a peculiar type of occupational control rather than an expression of the inherent nature of particular occupations. A profession is not, then, an occupation, but a means of controlling an occupation' (1972, p. 45). He also goes on to redefine professionalization as an historical process rather than a process that particular occupations undertake because of their 'essential' qualities.

Johnson's is typical of what is now termed the 'power approach' to the professions. He recognized the explanatory weaknesses of the trait approach. I therefore wish to explore these traits but I will do so in context, looking at their evolution over time.

The knowledge monopoly

This characteristic believes that professional journalists acquire certain skills and knowledge that distinguish them from non-professionals. The legendary *Guardian* investigative journalist David Leigh is among many when he cites the power to report objectively as evidence for the enduring need for trained, skilled reporters:

> We're not talking 'unmediated media' here. We're talking about corrupted media. And the online world, with its don't-pay, something-for-nothing mentality, is very vulnerable to lies and propaganda.
>
> (Leigh, 2007)

Journalists on both sides of the Atlantic insist that objectivity gives them professional status, especially when they feel threatened by others practising journalism. Objectivity is a slippery term, encompassing certain established codes such as non-partisanship, balance and detachment as opposed to bias. It emerged as a driving principle in the early part of the last century. There is, of course, much debate within media studies and branches of philosophy as to whether objectivity is humanly possible (McNair, 2005; Gaukroger, 2012). But within the industry, the term is generally understood to denote the need for editorial staff to keep their own views out of their reporting and offer a multiply sourced, balanced picture. Those who ardently defend the industry's professional boundaries assert that balance requires seasoned skill and judgement which only those who have been trained, tutored or at least thoroughly immersed in newsroom traditions can muster. However, these claims often rely on a concept of objectivity that is now over a century old.

Objectivity did not just suddenly emerge as a journalistic mantra. Its arrival coincided with the drive by proprietors to be seen as upholding professional high standards of practice to quell concerns about muckraking, chequebook journalism and sensationalism. In the late eighteenth century, the emerging economics of mass production and distribution in the United Kingdom and United States offered media owners both the beginnings of the profit incentive dominant today and the possibility of breaking free of political control and asserting their independence. Until this time, most newspapers had been politically partisan, dependent to varying extents on party patronage. Massive new presses could print thousands of copies of a newspaper every hour to feed increased circulation, and the ability to illustrate newspapers strengthened their appeal. The growing public demand for a steady stream of news forced proprietors to develop the first 'professional' newsrooms.

In journalism, it was specifically the notion of objectivity that helped to differentiate the practice as professional as it allowed editors to distance themselves from patronage and party politics. American authors in particular have identified objectivity as a key element of the professional self-perception of journalists (see Schudson, 1978 and 2001; Reese, 1990; Ognianova and Endersby, 1996; Mindich, 1998). The end of restrictive taxation in 1855 was a significant moment in promoting neutrality and impartiality as the basis of news provision. While editors did not rule out favouring one political party over another, that decision would be made by the papers themselves rather than forced by economic considerations (Chalaby, 1998, pp. 130–3).

Objectivity, or the desire for it, coupled with the idea that journalists were in pursuit of the 'truth' also influenced the routinization of news production (Tuchman, 1972). The processes and practices of journalism focused on presenting a complete picture, with all the facts, in order to achieve objectivity. American sociologist Gaye Tuchman has described the news-making process as a series of 'strategic rituals' aimed at achieving objectivity:

> They [editors] assume that, if every reporter gathers and structures 'facts' in a detached, unbiased, impersonal manner, deadlines will be met and libel suits avoided.
>
> (1972, p. 664)

But one of the problems with establishing journalism as a profession is that the concept of objectivity may be illusory, subject to institutional and sociocultural mores over time. Take, for example, the selection of sources. In journalism, it is often felt that by representing two sides of a debate, objectivity is achieved. But are there only ever two sides to a story? Some stories may involve many viewpoints and not constitute a clear-cut binary. Second, the availability of sources must adhere to newsroom routines – those who are available and articulate at deadline time will be the ones used.

Therefore, while it might certainly be seen that objectivity distinguishes the media professional, paid journalists have no more monopoly on that concept than any other citizen, especially given the economic prerogative of the organizations many work within. It is an oft-cited adage that a reporter is only as good as their next story or their sources. While journalists may enjoy the credibility and status that being a paid professional brings, they have no more ownership of that knowledge than that which being part of an organization or a well-known brand brings.

Exclusivity

The second trait of a profession is that its borders are well defined, with a clear demarcation between professional and non-professional practitioners. Journalism is keen to establish boundaries between 'professional' journalism and that practised by unpaid citizens such as bloggers. The industry and its practitioners at times fiercely defend the exclusivity of their occupational ideology. Durkheim (1957) viewed professions as moral communities whose shared commitment to, and ritual reaffirmations of, sets of shared norms served to define, promote and police group membership. To its members, journalism constitutes an occupation of particular public significance, reliant upon independent autonomy, requiring specific skills, knowledge, training, production techniques and specific ethical commitments.

Journalism has, in fact, only been a paid occupation for a relatively short time in its long history. When the first printing presses were set up by William Caxton in the late fifteenth century, a key moment in the development of mass media, the writers made little income because copyright lay with the publishers. Instead, authors and journalists relied on patronage for earnings rather than making a living in their own right. Though the status of authors was incrementally improved over time by acts of parliament which established property rights for authors, few journalists could make even a basic living from the activity. Their work was regarded as akin to novelists and political theorists, subject to the whims of partisan publishers rather than a means to a regular income. Even great literary figures, such as Charles Dickens, undertook their significant and respected journalism beside their creative and more profitable endeavours.

History shows how fundamental changes to the commercial base of journalism impact on the occupational status of its practitioners. The nineteenth century saw dramatic developments in journalism, which had far-reaching effects as resonant as any of the recent changes wrought by the Internet. Major advances in printing and in paper-making technology led to rapid growth in the newspaper industry and the emergence of the penny press, mass-circulation newspapers that an ordinary member of the public could afford to buy. Until this time, newspapers were funded by yearly subscription, paid in full and in advance – something only the wealthy élite could afford. However, increasing industrialization created new audiences that warranted adding the term 'mass' to media. Modernity drew people from the country into employment in cities. Thanks to these dramatic political and demographic shifts, and rising literacy levels, newspaper owners found a new market for their products, offering the public an ever-present supply of cheap and interesting reading matter, sold on street corners by newspaper boys.

Despite the growing interest in international affairs, newspapers were still regional and local until the mid-nineteenth century, largely due to the logistics of production and distribution. Horace Greeley's *New York Tribune*, launched in 1841, changed this. The appeal of his title beyond New York was secured by his illustrious staff (which for a short time included the revolutionary socialist thinker Karl Marx) and his campaigning liberalism, which heralded the identification of the journalist as a crusader. Under Greeley's leadership, the *Tribune*, circulated by rail and steamboat lines, became the first newspaper to unite the country in the mission to abolish slavery. Later, during the American Civil War, Greeley transported thousands of copies of the *Tribune* to other cities. And in 1886, the *Tribune* took a further technological leap by becoming the first newspaper to adopt Ottmar Mergenthaler's linotype machine, rapidly increasing the speed and accuracy with which type could be set. The Linotype machine allowed printers to set a line of type at once, using the machine's 90-character keyboard. Because the one-character-at-a-time Gutenberg process was so slow, for more than 400 years after the press's invention, most newspapers consisted of eight pages or fewer. With the advent of the Linotype, that quickly changed. As editors overcame logistical problems, they became keen to expand their news coverage and required skilled practitioners.

The invention of the telegraph (by Samuel Morse in 1837) boosted the speed and reliability of reporting by enabling the swift transfer of information from one source to another, even from one country to another. A new type of news provider emerged to supply the demand for coverage of international affairs. Major news agencies, known commonly as 'wire' services, originated in France in 1835 with the founding of Agence Havas, which later became Agence France Presse (AFP). Its founder, Charles-Louis Havas, is described on AFP's website as 'the father of global journalism'. In 1848, six large New York papers set up a co-operative, or pool system, to provide stakeholders with coverage of events in Europe, rather than each newspaper suffering the expense of placing dedicated staff overseas. This arrangement was later formalized into the Associated Press, which received the first-ever transmission of European news through the transatlantic cable. Information that had previously taken ten days to be transported by ship between America and Europe could now be transferred in a few minutes.

As technology transformed the speed of newspaper production and lowered its costs, it served to professionalize and formalize the nature of journalism. Because telegraphs often broke down, sometimes a reporter was cut off before they had finished sending their story. To alleviate the problems caused by this, reporters developed the 'inverted pyramid' form, which involved stating the most pertinent facts at the beginning of the transmission. Thus, the most significant part of the story would probably reach the newspaper and if the latter part failed to get through, it would not ruin the story. Telegraph and cable transmission also required much tighter, more concise sentences and paragraphs, in contrast to the more literary style of earlier newspapers. Journalists had to recount their story in as few words as possible, to pack in the maximum facts. This approach persists in news reporting today, not only in newspapers but also in broadcast and online journalism. The reporter gets straight to the crux of the story, spelt out in the first short, attention-grabbing, concise paragraph. Although journalism is a form of storytelling and can employ similar dramatic devices, journalists must not wait to deliver a *dénouement*: the reader has to be told the essential facts at the outset.

It was as a result of mass mediation, and the need to deliver news quickly and in a uniform format, that clear job demarcations developed. But in the digital age, the situation has changed once more, presenting journalists with some challenges to protecting and distinguishing their role. Editors now look for candidates who are adept at multi-tasking, capable of presenting stories in different formats. It would appear that the more skills you have the more you are viewed as a true professional. It is not that those skills are in any way monopolized by journalists; they could be acquired by anyone. It is the fact that a professional journalist can operate at speed in a context of convergence that distinguishes them. The requisite skills are constantly increasing – it is no longer enough to have seasoned judgement and a grasp of search-engine optimization. The ability to code in HTML is now becoming a highly prized prerequisite in some quarters.

The Internet is creating new roles that employ the skills of journalism but in non-journalistic contexts. Examples would be in campaigning, such as the work of non-governmental organizations or individuals in the promotion of particular concerns either through the mainstream media or through their own means. Public relations and marketing firms also increasingly employ former journalists and utilize many of the techniques once 'owned' by media professionals. So, it is very difficult to see journalism as an exclusive profession when the skills and the techniques are learnt and adopted by individuals and occupations outside the media industry.

Professional bodies

A professional association or society is an organization created to support a specific profession. Certain standards are upheld. Many professional bodies offer accreditation via membership that can be a requirement of being allowed to practise certain professions. For example, the General Medical Council registers doctors to practise medicine in the United Kingdom. The Bar Council is the professional body for barristers in England and Wales. It provides representation and services for the Bar, as well as guidance on issues of professional practice. Likewise, if you want to work as an engineer in the United States, you first need an engineering licence from an approved body.

At present, journalists do not need any form of professional accreditation to practise. Nonetheless, journalism has sought to mirror the traits of law and medicine by establishing organizations to promote and safeguard the interests of the sector, ranging from trades unions designed to protect the interests of workers and foster higher professional standards to associations seeking to reflect the interests of owners and influence national media policy. For example, in the United Kingdom, The Chartered Institute of Journalists claims to be the oldest professional body for journalists in the world. It was founded – as the National Association of Journalists – in 1884 and six years later was granted its Royal Charter by Queen Victoria, to protect and serve those employed in the field of journalism. However, unlike membership of the British Medical

Association, which is taken as evidence of a doctor's ability to practice, membership of journalism associations has no such bearing on professional status. Similarly, the Newspaper Society represents and promotes the interests of Britain's regional and local media. It was founded in 1836 and is believed to be the oldest publishers' association in the world. The sector is focused on providing local news and information across its 1,100 daily and weekly, paid-for and free newspaper titles, and 1,600 websites. The Society of Editors was formed by a merger of the Guild of Editors and the Association of British Editors in April 1999 and represents editors in all sectors of the media. A key objective of the society is to support and maintain self-regulation of the Press.

Trades unions, such as the National Union of Journalists (NUJ) in the United Kingdom founded in 1907, helped establish distinct training routes, employment terms and job descriptions. But over time, through the gradual corporatization of the media, particularly since the mid-1980s, the role and power of trades unions have declined. Declining unionization was one of the most significant features of the British labour market in the 1980s. In general, the proportion of British establishments that recognized trades unions for collective bargaining over pay and working conditions fell by almost 20 per cent between 1980 and 1990 (Millward et al., 1992). Nygren has explored the declining membership of the Swedish Union of Journalists to see whether this has any consequences for the notion of journalism as a separate field within media production. 'Trade unions are important institutions for the profession of journalism. A profession needs institutions like the unions to control and develop the profession; they are a tool to produce social closure toward other occupations and to safeguard the standards of the profession' (Nygren, 2011, p. 207).

While Nygren argues that weaker unions might be the sign of a reverse development, a de-professionalization of journalism, media organizations and the journalism occupation have nonetheless gone to pains to delineate clear perimeters between professional and non-professional practitioners. Thurman (2008) charted the varying ways in which formal media organizations formulate mechanisms for managing user-generated content.[2]

Education and training

One of the common characteristics of professions is that they are closed ranks, with a strong emphasis on training. In 1900, there was no such thing as a journalism training school or qualification. By the end of the

First World War, nearly every major journalism school in the United States had been established, often at the behest of newspaper owners. Education has been one of the biggest factors in the determination of journalism as a profession. It has signalled three things:

1 It has coincided with, even enabled, the breakdown of the power of trades unions, such as the NUJ, which ensured clear demarcations and uniformity in the training, job descriptions and working conditions for journalists.
2 The industry has done so by increasingly putting the onus on would-be journalists to fund their own training and education pre-entry, creating a filtering system in universities and colleges.
3 Shifting the training of journalists to the university sector reveals the industry desire – and indeed its practitioners' – to be viewed as highly qualified, skilled and more able to help defend the borders of the occupation.

As mentioned, journalism was once viewed as and trained in the manner of a trade. Training for a trade in European cultures has been a formal tradition for many centuries. A tradesperson typically begins as an apprentice, working for and learning from a master, and after a number of years is released from his/her master's service as a journeyman. After a journeyman has proven him/herself to his trade's guild, he/she may settle down as a master and work for him/herself, eventually taking on his/her own apprentices.

Since the start of the twentieth century, this process has been changed in many ways. A tradesperson still begins as an apprentice, but the apprenticeship is carried out partly through working for another tradesperson and partly through attending an accredited trade school for a pre-defined period of time, after which he/she is fully qualified. Starting one's own business is purely a financial matter, rather than being dependent on status. Few trades still make a distinction between a qualified tradesperson and a master. While a recognized qualification is mandatory for an individual to register as a tradesperson in some countries, it is not the case in others.

As the next chapter describes, in some countries this was how most journalists learnt their 'trade' until as recently as the late twentieth century. The teaching and evaluation of journalism practice, for instance, has traditionally had its routes in 'on-the-job' training or at tertiary colleges. Journalism training in the 1960s and 1970s emphasized core skills of reporting and writing. A reporter wishing to move into production journalism, such as sub-editing or layout, would learn these skills through on-the-job training. Sub-editing was seen as a senior journalistic task to be undertaken by those with considerable reporting experience.

This changed with the technological developments in the early to mid-1980s, specifically with the rise of desktop publishing, which enabled many of the once-separate journalism roles to be merged. But in the past 20 years, it has increasingly become a graduate profession for which pre-entry preparation is gained as part of a bachelor's or master's degree.

If a media occupation such as journalism were simply a trade, then only vocational training would be required. The entry profile suggested by the industry's shifting preferences suggests otherwise. It is notoriously difficult to break into the media, candidates requiring either significant pre-entry postgraduate training and qualifications or considerable insider access – usually both. It follows that, with greater training requirements, it should get easier to vet and weed out those who do not fit with the industry's profile and priorities.

Basic journalism training today might typically encompass technical skills as well as an underpinning in the essential craft of reporting, mirroring the demand for multi-skilled entrants who can function at a very high level. This contrasts greatly with the idea that trainees would gain the rudimentary skills before entry and then be coached and mentored by senior staff. Today, the trainees may operate virtually unilaterally in their first position.

It is interesting that some high-profile training establishments and universities continue to refer to journalism in terms of its professional characteristics and promote themselves on the basis of the number of leading figures they employ. The assumption here is that the most-valued journalists are those who fit a fairly narrow and elite definition of what constitutes a professional journalist. This professionalization of journalism education also serves to disconnect students and trainees from their own individual potential, as it requires them to leave any preconceptions 'at the door' and hand themselves over to 'canons of professional expertise' (Carey, 1980, p. 6) as embodied in the might of 'famous' lecturers.

Others have recently emphasized both historical and recent attempts by employers to exercise influence over professional education in order to promote instrumentalist training agendas and to de-emphasize, or altogether remove, critical aspects from journalism courses (Reese, 1999; Reese and Cohen, 2000).

Codes

Efforts to professionalize journalism began in earnest in the early twentieth century in response to the sensationalism and distortion that accompanied the commercialization of the Press in the latter part of the 1800s as the proprietors competed to enlarge their readership. Better printing technology and faster transmission speed also spurred this competition to increase their circulation and obtain more advertising revenue. Charles Anderson Dana of the *New York Sun* (1861), a former city editor to Horace Greeley, articulated for the growing industry the now universal description of what makes news: 'man bites dog' not 'dog bites man'. That is, if it is to attract and interest large audiences, news should convey out-of-the-ordinary events rather than the predictable and everyday ones. In the mid-1890s, Joseph Pulitzer (in the *New York World*) and William Randolph Hearst (in the *San Francisco Examiner* and later the *New York Morning Journal*) transformed newspapers, with sensational and scandalous news coverage, drawings and features such as comic strips.

Professional journalism was the solution to the crisis, it was felt. It was a revolutionary idea that the owner and editor of a newspaper would be split, and a 'Chinese Wall' put between them. News would no longer be shaped to suit the partisan interests of press owners, but rather would be determined by trained non-partisan professionals, using judgement and skills honed in journalism schools.

The move to professionalization has always gone hand in hand with concerns about falling standards. The first British Royal Commission on the Press (1949) suggested that the editorial production of newspapers should be regarded as a profession, stating that the professional relationship is between the newspaper as professional provider and the readership as its client:

> The direct relationship is between the newspaper and the reader, and the responsibility is shared among all those who serve and shape the newspaper's personality, whether they are individual proprietors, directors, managers or writing journalists. We should like to see all those who share this responsibility regard themselves as members of a single profession.
>
> (1949, p. 169)

Codes of ethics and practice have been established in the media in a similar way to those for doctors and lawyers. Legendary journalist Walter

Lippmann urged journalists to find a code of ethics to self-regulate the newspaper industry and guard against abuses in his 1920 book, *Liberty and the News*. His entreaty followed similar moves, in the United States, by the American Medical Association and the American Bar Association soon after their formation. Without robust self-regulation, Lippmann warned, the Press faced legislation that would severely restrict their activities. This drive tied in with wider discussions about journalistic procedure, the social responsibility of the Press and the publication of some of the first books on media ethics (Tumber and Pentoulis in De Burgh, 2005, p. 65). The American Society of Newspaper Editors (ASNE), founded in 1922, was the first professional media body to adopt a formal code, followed by what is now one of the biggest professional journalism bodies in the United States, the Society for Professional Journalists in 1926.

In the United Kingdom, the trade union the NUJ was founded to protect the working conditions of its members and end financial hardship. Initially, the NUJ did not work towards forging an ethical code, in contrast with another UK body, the Institute of Journalists, which threatened to expel any member who ignored theirs. However, by the first Royal Commission on the Press in 1947, the NUJ sought to elevate the status of journalism to that of established professions by declaring a drive to raise standards: 'We seek above all else, as a body of professional men and women, that the industry in which we serve the community should be directed and managed primarily in the public interest' (cited in Elliott, 1978, p. 176). Though a later Commission in 1977 has a single paragraph on 'professionalism' which states 'it is not realistic to expect journalism to become a profession in the sense that only people licensed by a national body at a national level may practice' (1977, para. 18.3).

Print media in the United Kingdom are not subject to any specific statutory controls on their content and activities, other than the general criminal and civil law. Rather, the Press ostensibly regulates itself, through the Press Complaints Commission (PCC) – an independent, non-statutory body that is responsible for maintaining the Editorial Code of Practice and investigating complaints into alleged breaches of the Code. By virtue of its status, the PCC has no powers to impose penalties on those it finds guilty of breaches.

The Code consists of 16 clauses: on accuracy, the opportunity for reply, respect for privacy, harassment, intrusion into shock or grief, the interests of children, the protection of children in sex cases, entry into hospitals, the reporting of crime, the use of clandestine devices and subterfuge, the protection of victims of sexual assault, discrimination, financial journalism, the protection of confidential sources, payment for information relating to criminal trials and payments to criminals. Most of the restrictions outlined in the Code are subject to a 'public interest' test, under which a restriction does not apply, if, when challenged by the PCC, an editor can show that publication contributed to the detection or prevention of a crime, the protection of public health and safety and – most significantly – preventing the public from being misled by the statements or actions of an individual or organization.

Statutory controls on freedom of the Press are widely regarded as an unreasonable restriction on freedom of speech and, as such, of democratic rights.[3] However, the activities of some irresponsible elements in the Press, and the PCC's weakness in enforcing its Code, have frequently generated considerable support for legislation.[4] The threat of regulation is believed to encourage restraint and good practice. Broadcast media, by contrast, are already subject to extensive statutory regulations. Today, these are largely set out in the Communications Act 2003 and enforced by the Office of Communications (Ofcom). The BBC is regulated by its Royal Charter obligations. The PCC has been widely criticized as ineffective partly because it is incapable of keeping the Press in check, as it is funded by the newspaper industry (via the Press Standards Board of Finance). The PCC and its supporters deny this, emphasizing the Commission's independence and the majority of lay members on its board.

At the time of writing, the PCC has confirmed that it will be reformed in response to criticism following the phone-hacking scandal. This follows the recommendations of Lord Justice Leveson. It has become quite evident to critics of the PCC that the existence of journalistic codes of practice in them do not denote a profession. Unlike medics, journalists who breach the code do not face being struck off, nor do those who err face major fines or other punishments. Codes are based on a consensual model of self-regulation which has proven difficult to measure and enforce.

It is possible that the Press will come under a single, more stringent regulatory umbrella akin to Ofcom, which oversees the Broadcasting Code as stipulated by the Communications Act 2003. Ofcom, for instance, was able to fine the BBC a record £150,000 for broadcasting 'gratuitously offensive, humiliating and demeaning' prank telephone calls made by Russell Brand and Jonathan Ross to the actor Andrew Sachs in October 2008.

Doing good work

Notwithstanding the lack of a unified regulatory system for all areas of the journalistic media, the ideal of social responsibility has served to foster a shared identity and culture among journalists and has served as a measure of its efficacy. This ideal is particularly salient when we consider how both news organizations and journalists themselves promote the notion of the public good to defend their respective positions. On the breaking news of the UK phone-hacking scandal, journalist Ros Wynne-Jones wrote a column for the *Independent* passionately defending the sector as working ultimately for its readers:

> At its best, tabloid journalism is an old skill, a trade in the old-fashioned sense that has been traditionally learned through apprenticeship in the newsroom. It is part instinct, part training. Most hacks also possess a naturally deep disdain for authority, establishment and big business. I have seen some reporters squeeze through lavatory windows, lock themselves in broom cupboards, blag their way onto flights and don hilarious disguises. Getting the story is everything – indeed, too much so in some of the circumstances now emerging.[5]

Based on interviews with tabloid journalists, Deuze (2005a, p. 878) has noted that '[j]ournalists in the more entertaining sector of the media share notions of ethical sensibilities, servicing the public, editorial autonomy and public credibility in order to position themselves as a distinctive genre'.

He argues that it is more productive to think of journalism's self-determination as an occupational ideology than as a profession. Indeed, research by Russo (1998) suggests that journalists identify themselves more easily with the profession of journalism than with the medium or media company that employs them.

Golding and Elliott (1979), Merritt (1995) and, more recently, Kovach and Rosenstiel (2001) describe the ideology of journalism as

- *Public service*: journalists provide a public service (as watchdogs or 'news-hounds', active collectors and disseminators of information);
- *Objectivity*: journalists are impartial, neutral, objective, fair and (thus) credible;
- *Autonomy*: journalists must be autonomous, free and independent in their work;

- *Immediacy*: journalists have a sense of immediacy, actuality and speed (inherent in the concept of 'news');
- *Ethics*: journalists have a sense of ethics, validity and legitimacy.

Aldridge and Evetts (2003) posit professionalism in journalism as a discourse rather than a set of quantitative features (p. 548). This makes sense as a means for stability and control of an industry going through dynamic changes. It is a powerful form of self-determination and discipline shared by managers and workforce alike. Journalism no longer resists this discourse, indeed the Leveson Inquiry has strikingly shown how the media industry seeks legitimacy and tries to distance itself from those within its fold who do not demonstrate the discourses of professionalism.

Conclusion: The professional journalistic identity

Journalism clearly constitutes an occupation of particular public significance whose importance is generally recognized; whose successful performance depends upon maintaining an independent autonomy; and which necessarily involves particular skills, knowledge, training, production techniques and specific ethical commitments.

This chapter has shown that the traditional class divisions once used to divide tradespeople such as plumbers, gas fitters and brewers from professionals – blue collar versus white collar – are largely irrelevant in the context of the media in the twenty-first century. Working in the media today requires no fixed entry route or standard qualifications. It combines a raft of technical, knowledge-based and administrative skills. Salaries and terms of employment vary massively and membership of collective bodies and trades unions is patchy.

Comparisons are made between journalism and more established and accepted professions such as law or medicine. Medics and lawyers are viewed as specialists delivering select services, having undergone a lengthy period of training in their field (Tunstall, 1973, p. 87; Henningham, 1979, p. 15). Paid journalists share a great deal in common with these professionals in terms of how they assert an essential set of skills and knowledge as prerequisites for a successful employment. These include areas such as legal expertise, reporting and writing protocols and a strong understanding of public affairs. In some cases, such as in the United Kingdom, shorthand, video and other technical skills are favoured. But, in addition to quantifiable skills and knowledge, media practice also brings to the fore a set of abstract attributes that are far harder to quantify within a checklist of professional criteria. They include initiative, flexibility and collegiality.

Defining media work as a trade is similarly challenging. Gas fitters, for example, must undergo cyclical assessments to retain their registration and can be de-registered if they are in breach of requirements. This does not happen to media workers. A journalist who breaches an ethical code might be reprimanded by their editor or even dismissed to set a public example. But they are quite likely to continue practising as a staff reporter or freelance for another publication. Similarly, an errant TV producer is not barred from finding work elsewhere even if their documentary landed a broadcaster with a libel writ. In contrast, tradespeople often have to adhere to European-wide or international standards, so cannot transfer their skills overseas if things go wrong at home.

Therefore, media practitioners do not fit easily into any category. A straw poll conducted in any newsroom or production house will find every candidate entered the workplace through different routes, with varying levels of qualifications and training and anticipating varied career trajectories. With the advent, first, of desktop publishing and, later, the Internet and other new media, plus the substantial reduction in the price of video and digital cameras, new 'alternative' routes have opened up too.

History has shown how professionalization has been used towards varying ends, such as protecting editorial independence, raising standards and lending credibility to a sector mired in muckraking tendencies. Professionalism meant that the news would appear the same whether the paper was owned by a Republican or a Democrat, Labour or Conservative. Professionalism would ensure that there was no longer cause for concern about the monopolistic nature of newspaper markets since owners would not abuse their power. Rather a seemingly deeper and a profiteering picture emerges from professionalization: if more media outlets in the same community merely reproduce the same professional content, fewer are needed, thus reinforcing the might of the big corporations over that of the small independents. Commentators such as Larson (1977) support the view that the process of professionalization ultimately served to promote and maintain the profit-motive rather than to raise the status of practitioners. As the scale of media organizations grew, often merging to form corporations or conglomerates, so there were fewer rivals battling for supremacy, while with fewer players it was easier to control the competitive environment.

At the same time, employers could use professionalization for their own ends to displace the cost of investing in workplace training onto employees, to exploit the commitment to the delivery of a vital public service by increasing workplace demands without pay increases or paid overtime and to deploy the claim that they offer a product or service delivered by independent professionals to enhance their market value. But that does not answer the question as to why journalists themselves embraced and promoted the notion of being part of a distinct profession. As the boards of media corporations faced the challenge of maintaining the efficiency of large numbers of people sometimes over vast geographical areas, this issue was solved by the rise of the manager in newsrooms. Journalists on the whole tended to accept this, and still do, as they could see that they relied on the business model to survive. While employees within large organizations could not determine their own conditions of employment, professionalism nevertheless provided a basis upon which such workers could lay claim to a particular class status, articulate demands that they be afforded the respect and remuneration from their employers that their status demanded, and even assert a degree of independent influence over their own working conditions.

However, while editorial staff felt compelled for professional reasons to split themselves off ideologically from the business side of media and the commercial imperative was universally viewed as in conflict with editorial independence, it was generally accepted. In fact, during debates over the continued viability of the journalistic media in the digital age, journalists seem to oppose the idea of state ownership or funding of the Press, arguing it would be anathema to professional independence.

Significantly, Marjoribanks (2000) has shown how journalists' self-identification as respectable 'white collar' workers, a professional identity defined by contrast to 'blue collar' print workers, has been crucial to the relative lack of opposition to workplace transformations that have led to both large-scale redundancies and effective de-unionization of newspaper production environments. Businesses, in turn, have proved willing, initially, to share the benefits of commercial gain with their employees. Employees were able to profit personally particularly towards the late twentieth century when they were offered share options, in the major corporations that owned the media, as incentives.

The professionalization of the media has also gone hand in hand with technological advances. It is commonplace today for journalists to claim that technological changes have led to the demise of professional model of journalism because they allow unpaid amateurs to participate. However, over time, news proprietors have embraced technological development as the means to increase profits and speed up news production. For example, the introduction of the telegraph as a means to transmit copy back to newsrooms in the early twentieth century brought about the economy of language – short sentences and paragraphs – we have become accustomed to in news.

But in the second decade of the new millennium the commercial buoyancy of professionalized journalism has now declined, with newsrooms closing down, resources stripped and staff laid off. Seeing this scenario, journalism might better be regarded as a semi-profession for two reasons. First, we can no longer exclude non-professionals from the field in the digital age. Second, it would go against the grain of free expression to entirely locate journalism within a closed, regimented domain.

What 'professionalization' represents is *not* the establishment of a 'profession' with definitive qualities, but rather the mobilization of both particular claims regarding the professional status of journalism itself (or, at least, some areas of it) and the deployment of particular techniques to promote 'professionalism'.[6]

In Chapter 2, we will examine whether the typical education and training routes into the media properly prepare entrants for their future careers.

2 Preparing Media Professionals

As we saw in Chapter 1, the size and nature of the journalistic talent pool has transformed in the last 30 years. With the decline of professional bodies and the expansion in university media courses, there is now no single ideal route into the media. This presents a very confusing picture for anyone hoping to enter the field. A straw poll in any production company or newsroom will elicit many different accounts of how employees achieved their position. For some, it will be down to a lucky opportunity, a chance meeting perhaps. For others, it might have resulted from years of training and internships or a long period of education. Each individual believes their way is preferable. So which route is best?

The backgrounds of typical media recruits have changed considerably over the past 30 years. As discussed in the previous chapter, this has been one of the main indicators of a shift towards a professionalized media. There has been a rapid rise in graduate intake and, as degree courses proliferate, a demand for postgraduate qualifications. On the one hand, some commentators have poured scorn on what they describe as 'Mickey Mouse' media degrees. Universities are being urged by some in the media to overhaul or close degree courses that are failing to prepare young people for work, warning of a 'mismatch' between graduates' skills and the demands of employers. On the other, studies have shown that graduates, especially from top universities, have an advantage over school leavers. Either way, employers have noted a dearth of skills and attributes in many graduates, a fact that makes it harder for would-be journalists to know where to find the best career preparation.

There is currently a multi-tiered system of journalism education in place with programmes at sub-degree, degree and postgraduate degree level. This reflects the variety within journalism work and the different levels at which it is practised. Courses vary in length from weekend tasters to three-year degrees, and are offered both within the state education sector and by private companies. Journalism training is also provided in-house by major media organizations, such as the BBC College of Training, often as a formal scheme for the induction of new trainees and also for the ongoing refreshment and updating of skills and knowledge. Andrew Gilligan's actions in the David Kelly affair were often framed by the fact that he had moved from print to broadcast journalism. As a consequence, after the Hutton Inquiry, the BBC responded by developing a raft of new training courses for all its staff via a newly formed BBC College of Journalism. In-service training such as this and the legal refresher courses that newsrooms often send reporters on are seen as not only enhancing performance but also sending signal to staff the need for occupational commitment.

From its beginnings in the United States, journalism education has focused on preparing students to work in professional media organizations. In his aforementioned book, *Liberty and the News* (1920), Lippmann bemoaned the fact that American journalists were doing the work of 'preachers, revivalists, prophets and agitators'. They reported the news 'by entirely private and unexamined standards'. Nations that thought themselves to be self-governing 'provided no genuine training schools for the [journalists] upon whose sagacity they were dependent'. In-depth preparation should be a requirement for the job, he said, and that training should be akin to science, which had successfully harnessed the 'discipline of modernized logic'. Decades later, Bill Kovach and Tom Rosenstiel were still pursuing the same possibly elusive end, encouraging news people to adopt the rigor of their five 'intellectual principles of a science of reporting' (2001, p. 78).

Even if a science of journalism remains obscure, Lippmann's quest for every journalist to be pre-educated in the mores of the newsroom has largely been achieved. Nearly a century on, so many young people are graduating in journalism, communications and media that some form of university pre-entry degree seems to have become a prerequisite for a reporting or editing job. Originally, the focus was on preparing candidates to enter newspapers, then, as new media forms emerged, specialist programmes were launched in broadcast journalism to cater for what were felt to be the specificities of radio and television. Over time, as technology has developed and businesses operating on the periphery of journalism have expanded, courses have been introduced in applying journalism skills to related professional areas including advertising, public relations and media management.

Simultaneously, the globalization of media and the growth of journalism in emerging democracies have created an international demand for Western-style news reporting and editing techniques. Universities report unprecedented numbers of applications for places on journalism courses in the West from India, China, Africa and the Middle East, areas with nothing like the journalistic or political-cultural history of North America or Western Europe. The global reach and impact of brands such as the BBC, Bloomberg and Hearst have inspired a desire for immersion in Western styles and systems.

Ironically, the massive global expansion and systematization of journalism as a higher education course coincides with widespread doubt about the future of mainstream journalism on all fronts – technical, professional and, not least, commercial. All this signals an explicit challenge to any notion of a 'canon' of media training. Whereas in the United States, Lippmann's legacy is that it is widely accepted that journalists will attend a J-school prior to launching their careers, in the United Kingdom there are mixed feelings about the more recent shift from on-the-job or tertiary training to university schooling in news values. The one overarching theme is that of a desire to professionalize journalism by creating an ontology, epistemology or 'science' of journalism as Lippman and his supporters proposed.

Coinciding with the shift to graduate entry has been sharp debate inside journalism as well as within the academy, about how – and even whether – to educate and train. There are acute tensions within newsrooms and among academic colleagues about the relevance and appropriateness of journalism taught in universities and the about conduct of media research.

The question for educators, the industry and future practitioners must be what skills and knowledge do the new generation of media practitioners actually need in order to thrive in the digital age? Are these the same skills that have served journalists well over the decades – the fundamental 'nuts and bolts' of newsgathering? Or do we need a radically different approach to equip digitally savvy information providers with the means to knowingly navigate a highly dynamic new media landscape?

Development of training and education models

Until the last 30 or 40 years, journalism was viewed as a trade or craft requiring a formal indenture period with a local newspaper. A school leaver would be assigned rudimentary administrative tasks while they gradually learned 'the ropes' from more senior staff. Often, the school leaver's first job was 'copy boy' – for it was a predominantly male domain – which involved running from desk to desk with the typed news stories. The professional education of journalists in colleges began in earnest in the United States in the early twentieth century, commonly as part of a printing or English course (Weaver and Wilhoit, 1986, pp. 41–4). Legendary journalist Joseph Pulitzer was a key instigator in the formalization of professional journalism training in his 1904 essay, 'Planning a School of Journalism' (Pulitzer, 1904). Pulitzer's argument was that journalists influence public discourse as information providers and social critics. As such, they themselves require a grounding in contextual knowledge or areas such as constitutional law, ethics, history and economics to fulfil their perceived role within a democratic society. While advocating skills and knowledge primarily geared towards professional practice, Pulitzer took a view that the approaches used in law and business, specifically case studies and critiques, would foster thoughtful practice. His endeavours initiated the launch of an undergraduate school of journalism at New York's Columbia University in 1912.

Media education became more formalized from the 1950s onwards in the United States and United Kingdom, both professionally and academically. The National Council for the Training of Journalists (NCTJ) was founded in 1951 to run the newspaper industry's training scheme, following the findings of a Royal Commission on the Press. Its 1949 report said:

> The problem of recruiting the right people into journalism, whether from school or from university, and of ensuring that they achieve and maintain the necessary level of education and technical efficiency, is one of the most important facing the Press, because the quality of the individual journalist depends not only on the status of the whole profession of journalism but the possibility of bridging the gap between what society needs from the Press and what the Press is at present giving it. The problem is the common interest and the common responsibility of proprietors, editors and other journalists.[1]

In the early days, indentured trainees studied at colleges of further education and were examined in the General Proficiency Test, taken at the end of the three-year training period. All trainees attended day-release classes at college.

From 1965, 'block release' courses were introduced and an experimental 'pre-entry' course was run. Year long pre-entry courses were developed further, followed by 18- and 20-week fast-track postgraduate courses and the accreditation of journalism postgraduate degree courses. The old 'Prof Test' was modernized and became the National Certificate Examination. More recently, the NCTJ has accredited three-year undergraduate degree courses that have a strong vocational content, in-company training schemes and courses delivered by private providers. Most new entrants to journalism in the United Kingdom now have some pre-entry training and very few are raw recruits.

However, it is the rise of media and communication studies in higher education since the 1960s, and the resulting promotion of a desire to learn about and participate in the media both professionally and as a consumer, that has led to a debate within and about journalism training. The study of media emerged in English departments as students and academics recognized film and television as worthy of scrutiny. Growing numbers of young people began to see media courses as a way into this exciting new occupation. This led to a desire to connect media courses with practical experience, the desire for which grew in proportion throughout the 1980s. Some of the brightest and best flocked to the more industry-facing polytechnics as opposed to universities where they could get their hands on equipment and gain access to tutors with industry connections. Polytechnics did not see vocationalism as problematic, and with their widening access policies and industry-facing approach they began to embrace critical practice both as a pedagogic approach and as a way to encourage more and more bright young people to register.

Journalism modules became more commonplace, reflecting the influence of groups and scholars such as Stuart Hall, the Glasgow Media Group and cultural theorists who directly addressed journalism, such as Jean Baudrillard and Jürgen Habermas. With a rapidly growing ontology and more students drawn to media programmes, it was inevitable that before long these one-off modules would turn into full degrees in journalism.

A further threat to the traditional forms of journalism training in the United Kingdom came in the late 1980s and 1990s when some newspaper groups withdrew from the NCTJ to set up their own training schemes or chose to transfer to the National Vocational Qualifications (NVQ), which at the time attracted public funding. Professional news organizations were also looking to make efficiency savings by cutting the cost of training. Prior to this, a typical trainee joining a local newspaper would need in-house mentoring and intensive coaching, going on assignments with other reporters. In addition, they would be sent to classes to learn skills such as shorthand. Under union agreements built in to journalists' contracts, the company would shoulder the cost of sending the candidate on three-month-long block release programmes, covering fees and accommodation. Yet, often the benefits of this investment would be short-lived: the newly qualified journalists would swiftly gain promotion to a regional daily or evening paper or enter broadcasting.

The neo-Conservative emphasis in the 1980s also fostered individual zeal so that a growing number of new graduate entrants no longer considered local papers the apex of their ambition. The new news professionals saw the local media as a stepping stone. As a result, editors and companies began to think more strategically about cutting training costs or favouring candidates who came in with prior training over local, home-grown staff.

The changing face of the media was no longer reflected in the methods of the training bodies. The *Oxdown Gazette*, the fictional title for which all NCTJ trainees wrote during classes and exams, envisioned a roving reporter cycling about their district from vicar to school to fire station to pub. The consolidation of small, locally owned titles into big national and global corporations put an end to that way of working in local newsrooms. Paid-for broadsheet newspapers with decent but by no means guaranteed readerships were transformed into free-distribution tabloids carrying often 60 per cent advertising and 40 per cent editorial. An overarching title with umpteen localized editions might have once contained several hyper-local 'change pages', usually pages 1, 3, 5 and 7 featuring news specific to a fairly small locale. These were all but dispensed with, so that hyper-local audiences were delivered generic district-wide news on events and issues miles away. But because the paper was now free and delivered through letterboxes, readerships were guaranteed to advertisers notwithstanding readers' perceptions of quality.

Efficiency savings and the reduced need to get to the heart of hyper-local stories meant that fewer reporters were necessary and those that remained could work from their offices covering the major district-wide 'diary' stories such as council decisions and big-business announcements. Many of the larger media companies buying up local papers – for example, *Trinity Mirror* in the United Kingdom and *Gannett* in the United States – required staff to be skilled in areas such as writing branded copy for several titles in their company. For example, the *Trinity Mirror* scheme began to recruit university graduates unfamiliar with the area onto its daily morning and evening metropolitan titles rather than recruiting candidates from local newspapers with several years' experience and training. Their three-month scheme centred on them being able to write in different style for their morning and evening titles rather than having discrete staff in place on each title. In cities such as Liverpool, the *Daily Post* and sister evening title the *Liverpool Echo* were housed in the same building under the same company heading but were fiercely competitive, aiming to secure and protect their own exclusives. The new training system, however, focused on sharing content to save on resources, simply rebranding it for the different market segments each of the titles appealed to.

As traditional training routes ceased to prevail, there was a simultaneous shift in the university sector towards representing journalism as a set of professional skills and knowledges, not purely as a trade. This is one of the ways that the pre-1992 universities, and especially some of the most elite centres on both sides of the Atlantic, began to justify delivering what was once a trade as a profession. While the former polytechnics and new post-1992 universities still often align journalism, at least theoretically, with media, film and cultural studies, the 'old' universities have been far more determined to sever all ties with those disciplines, and have taken an academic position that is much closer to the US model. This model is preferred by the industry – the notion of teaching journalism 'as it is' rather than analysing journalism for its issues and effects.

University education in journalism

Educational provision for journalism also reflects views on its status, that is, whether it is regarded as a profession or as a craft or trade. It is in universities especially that journalism seems to fulfil the criteria required for a profession (Friedson, 2001). Promotional leaflets for degrees and Master's courses typically define journalism as an intellectual activity requiring specialized competence, autonomous practitioners informed about an ethical code reflecting its public service role. Journalism education in universities, by virtue of their status, tends to reflect the educational provision for other professions such as law.

Outside universities, such as in colleges, in-house media training schemes and private providers, journalism is more simply regarded as a craft or trade. Here, journalism education can and has been distilled to the acquisition of a set of skills. Even where its more professional qualities are recognized, it does not usually follow the normal knowledge-based models for the professional curriculum, instead aiming for applied knowledge or 'learning-by-doing'.

In the United Kingdom alone, figures from the Higher Education Statistics Agency indicate that 11,195 students took higher education courses in Journalism in 2010–2011; the figure for 2007–2008 was 9,220 and for 2006–2007, 8,995. In Media Studies, just under 29,000 students took higher education courses in 2010–2011. The total figure for HE students taking subjects within the area of Mass Communication and Documentation for 2010–2011 was 53,680. The Universities and Colleges Admissions Service (UCAS), the UK universities central admissions body, lists 505 journalism HE undergraduate programmes in the United Kingdom alone. In addition, dozens of providers, including colleges, universities and private firms, offer postgraduate training and education in journalism. In the university sector in particular, there is a huge variety in the modules and subjects that can be mixed and matched with journalism as part of a joint degree. Some students may choose to take their majority of credits in journalism but add, say, a foreign language, creative writing or a social science. Other students might study a 50–50 split of journalism with another subject which might be quite unconnected with the media. Business and history are typical examples. There is also a similar picture in the United States, which has many hundreds of journalism programmes and departments at all levels.

Herein lies a host of questions and issues. The sheer number of students gaining media qualifications has prompted concern, given the rapid contraction of jobs in mainstream journalism globally. There has been intense debate about the number of course providers and whether certain provision is appropriate preparation for a career. One position, the professional model of journalism education and training, is that the absence of an agreed framework for teaching journalism has hindered its development as a mature professional discipline in the Western world. Accordingly, media commentators have vociferously denounced theory-based courses on the basis that they are not practical enough, as if the only hallmark of a good course is if students get a mainstream journalism job after it. Inevitably, this debate has also led to calls for so-called 'Mickey Mouse' non-vocational media programmes to be closed. From another perspective, one which decouples media and journalism education from professional imperatives, the skills and critical knowledge gained on diverse academic programmes are relevant to a changing media landscape and are also highly transferrable to other sectors as well as to advanced scholarship.

Surveying undergraduate and postgraduate students in the United Kingdom, Hanna and Sanders (2010) surmise that undergraduates have more than one motivation for entering journalism which they partly attribute to the exuberance of youth. They also maintain that undergraduates bring diversity to newsrooms and are more willing to relate to the non-routine, unconventional and creative aspects of journalism than postgraduates are.

It is more productive to look for the themes that recur across journalism education than to identify the fissures. Three aspects of journalism that are typically covered – albeit in different weights and in different ways – are practice, context and theory. They are combined in varying proportions according to different educational models but nonetheless recur across the board. Their manifestations and incarnations in different educational and training contexts can be revealing in terms of media professionalism, as each situation can be analysed with regard to its particular relationship with, say, industry, culture, socio-political backdrop and so on. Before we look at that, let us define each point on this triangle.

Practical modules

Practice here refers to the acquisition and implementation of techniques and processes of journalism. Note that I did not say *the* techniques as that would suggest that a set of practices that had some sort of eternal primacy existed. The fact is it does not. Over time, techniques and processes have been shaped and nuanced by a host of internal and external factors as described and discussed in Chapter 1. Given the fact that practice is such a fluid and unfixed term, even within the blurred boundaries of a tradition such as journalism, the way it is approached in education and training speaks volumes about the particular inflections of those institutions.

The abiding training and education models used today tend to be based on journalism as a mass-produced industry with large general readerships and audiences, and, one which, as Mensing (2011) identifies 'embodies an understanding of communication as a process of transmission from producer to receiver' (2011, p. 15). Carey (2000) suggests that journalism education was initiated in the 'age of the reporter'. This would explain the fundamental emphasis on finding news and delivering it to a mass audience using widely practised techniques originating from the mechanization of journalism production, such as the inverted-pyramid approach, economical sentences and short paragraphs.

These fundamentals are enshrined as the marker of professional excellence. The economics of publishing mean those fixed, mainstream, industry-centric approaches are typical of the way students are taught and trained. There is an expectation that they will be equipped with the essential or, depending on level, threshold skills required to gain a foothold in the sector, work in another allied sector or independently beside it.

By their very nature, modules tend to be discrete, standalone learning units. Frequently, a module will be medium-specific, such as print, magazines, online, radio or TV. A module might also examine a particular journalistic process, such as sub-editing, news writing or features. One issue this immediately raises is whether programmes offer the opportunity for students to combine all these different aspects. In a real-world environment, these tasks and media do not exist in isolation but are melded and synthesized, requiring speed, flexibility and strong co-working to ensure optimum efficiency.

A further concern is that the pressure to teach an increasing number of technical skills leads to a decrease in other cognitive and knowledge-based modules. Given that these skills quickly become outdated, the question is whether it is appropriate to continue to educate journalism students in technicalities when what they really need are the ideas, creativity and ingenuity to know what to do with them. Moreover, should it not be the role of employers to impart technical skills when surely the purpose of a university education is to focus on cognitive and critical development?

A priority for any practical module is that it can equip students with the skills they need for their future in journalism. University and college quality assurance processes can mean significant delays and paperwork for academics seeking changes to their modules, which can affect the industry-responsiveness of courses. There is also the danger that staff-recruitment regulations may require academic experience over and above a current or recent newsroom background. In the United Kingdom, a study by a Sheffield University academic Tony Harcup revealed that universities could do more to help practitioners become research active.[2] While some universities offer their academic staff sabbaticals to work on updating their research, it would also be beneficial for staff teaching vocationally oriented modules to spend time in the industry updating their skills and knowledge.

Contextual modules

Journalism higher education courses usually deliver background knowledge and applied skills in a range of contexts again to signal their industry-facing nature. Journalists interact with, and are affected by, a host of contexts including legal frameworks, ethical and regulatory codes and formal and informal institutions. Similarly, journalism students may be interested in specializing in a particular area, such as science, the arts or crime. Equipping students with contextual knowledge also primes them for working in an industry that is based on processes and protocols. A glance through course prospectuses indicates that most programmes consider media law to be an essential area of contextual knowledge. The volume of law taught on courses has had to expand considerably because newsroom budgets can no longer sustain an on-site legal expert on smaller titles and outlets. Legal expertise is essential to protect the individual and their outlet from criminal prosecution for contempt, expensive civil action for libel and, perhaps most importantly, from loss of credibility (Hanna and Dodd, 2012). Another key course element is public affairs: journalists need to understand how political systems and governance operate at local, national and global levels. This is vital for reporters for three reasons: to be able to fulfil their consensual role as a watchdog for democracy, to be able to present complex issues accessibly and to know whom to interview on matters of public interest.

Contextual modules can cause difficulties. Students struggle to relate context learnt didactically in a classroom to the actual day-to-day practice of newsgathering and reporting. The question is what scope there is within the drive to achieve employability for to actively negotiate these contexts and challenge or at least to experiment with the efficacy of established reporting techniques. Despite this education in vital areas of context, journalists have gone on to commit serious errors, including allegations of phone hacking and failing to spot a banking crisis. Newsrooms urgently need to re-establish trust and faith in the way journalists cover these contextual areas. Interviewed for this book, one local news group editor said: 'Students come in thinking that the story is about the council, which is the biggest way to turn off readers. The story should be about people, with the council involvement being but one aspect of the story.' This places doubt on whether modular frameworks for delivering contexts and institutions, which require fact-based presentational knowledge on the part of students for assessment, might be missing the essence of how the public interact with major institutions. The danger is that well-qualified journalists may be entering newsrooms capable of speaking to officialdom and circumventing legal breaches, but they may not be best placed to understand the perspectives of their readers in order to serve as a vital bridge between citizens and institutions.

Ethics is also treated as a contextual module by many journalism training programmes, with a standalone unit on codes of practice and the moral principles of editorial behaviour and standards. This area of teaching has come under particular scrutiny in the United Kingdom during the Leveson Inquiry, with academics and the NCTJ being asked to submit statements on how ethics is taught at their institutions. Many are of the view that ethics should not be a separate module but should be integrated wholly into all modules, and learnt and embedded through practice. Others feel that the only way to signal the importance of ethics and standards is through a dedicated module.

Do standalone ethics models provide adequate preparation if they do not immerse students in real-world live scenarios? Then again, if students are only taught ethics in the heat of newsroom editorial decision-making, there is little space for them to reflect and to allow time and discussion for a considered approach. If ethics is only taught in an industry context, then industry pressures will surely influence the outcome. The fear is that contextual models deliver strategies in an abstract form, divorced from the reality of real-world journalism. They take a didactic approach that fails to put them to the test in context. They do not embrace the identity of intention of the individual journalist or the pressures they work under. This is why proponents of theoretically based studies of journalism believe students need to critically engage with the subject.

Theoretical modules

By 1920, the first departments of journalism emerged at the universities of Wisconsin and Missouri. A new approach to the study of journalism was introduced with a foundation in the field of communication studies by Wilbur Schramm soon after the Second World War; this challenged the boundaries between theory and practice and heralded closer academic scrutiny of media practice. Some, notably Carey (2000), have asserted that the study of communications may have downgraded the status of journalism practice and training:

> [B]y reading journalism functionally rather than intrinsically, it levelled journalism down to that of a signalling system while not

immeasurably increasing our understanding of journalism as a social act, a political phenomenon, and an imaginative construction of the social.

(Carey, 2000, pp. 20–1)

Industry leaders, and indeed some within higher education, have tended to mock the inclusion of theory on journalism programmes as irrelevant to modern-day newsroom routines. But advocates of theory – the ideas, suppositions, abstract concept of journalism that stand behind its practice – say that an academic critique of journalism is crucial to any undergraduate or postgraduate journalism programme to create an innovative, incisive, new generation of editors. According to critical approaches, practice has a basis in theory because it is a social construction that can only be properly understood by seeking to find the beliefs that lie behind it. Journalism education must go beyond the mastery of skills and the knowledge of values and standards if it is to adequately prepare graduates for a rapidly evolving media landscape. It must also provide graduates with a critical understanding of the notion of journalism itself in order to allow reflection on journalistic values, ethics and routines. Education has a serious contribution to make in this regard by ensuring that well-qualified entrants have a critical understanding of the important role journalism plays in society.

A start can be made by looking at the theorizing of other forms of practice, which has been defined as consisting of four dimensions: the intention of the practitioner, the interpretation of the activity by others and the historical and political context (Kemmis, 1998). Intuitively, this approach is sympathetic to the concerns of journalism. The emphasis thrown on the intention and interpretation of the activity highlights journalism's role and its relationship with the public. Similarly, the importance of the historical and political contexts of journalism practice is widely recognized and is in tune with the culture of journalism.

Teaching journalism students theory has prompted complaint that they will be ill prepared for the workplace, with resistance to the very notion of theory from some journalism lecturers. Frith and Meech (2007, p. 39) have pointed out 'a peculiar disjunction between the reality of how people did become journalists and the ideology of how they should become journalists, between the empirical evidence that journalism was now a career for graduates and the editorial suggestion that it should not be ....' The fact that journalism, an occupation that historically had not required formal training of the intellect beyond secondary school level, now expected its new recruits to have had some form of higher education could not be denied (2007, p. 139).

Journalists still express distrust of graduates. Richard Keeble (1998) cites former *Daily Star* Editor, Brian Hitchen, who commented: 'I've only met one graduate from journalism who was any good. Most of them are appalling. There's only one way to learn journalism and that's by starting at the bottom' (Keeble, 1998, p. 287). This development has impacted on 'traditional' university approaches through the encouragement of 'competence'- or 'outcome'-oriented learning as a hallmark of success in journalism education. Just as a student is considered to demonstrate 'competence' through the selection and application of appropriate solutions in accordance with professional expectations, journalism academics have tended to foster and defend industry-facing perspectives as the most authentic (Harcup, 2011).

Even within higher education, Tumber and Prentoulis identify a dichotomy between practice-led and theory-led approaches to best preparing students for the workplace:

> Some have experience as practitioners themselves and this focus on the vocation training of the students. Others come from recognized academic fields such as sociology, philosophy or political sciences and stress a non-vocational agenda, promoting research and intellectual endeavour.
>
> (2005, pp. 66–7)

That split is no longer so clear-cut, as universities commonly require practitioners to be research-active. The 'hackademic' is the new hybrid identity in journalism education, one-time pure practitioners who are moving into scholarly research and versing their students in critical practice (Niblock, 2007). The argument has been that the same research and analytical skills are used in journalism, as in academia, and this should be recognized. The difference is, however, that journalism practice, even at the highest level, does not advance our understanding and conception of journalism in the same way as academic research does. It is vital for this reason that research leading to the development of theory is pursued.

Issues

Socialization not education

Universities often act as recruitment departments for journalism firms. It is certainly quite common for editors to recruit students from particular courses. A symbiotic relationship between course provider and company occurs whereby the university benefits from the employability record of their cohorts and the company saves money on advertising and recruitment. But this also puts great pressure on universities to admit students on the basis of their perceived attractiveness to employers by the end of their courses. Some would argue that this goes against the grain of what universities are for – indeed their very name points to the need for diversity of intake and independence from commercial pressures. Increasingly, with the rise in tuition fees and the demand to publish the first destination of graduates from specific courses, admissions tutors feel under pressure to make employability judgements about 17-year olds and where they might be in three years' time.

Warren Breed, a former journalist turned sociologist, was one of the pioneers of the scientific study of news production. His professional experience of journalism led him to query how staff get to know and follow newsroom 'policy'. Breed (1955, p. 328) wrote:

> On being asked, they say they learn it 'by osmosis.' Sociologically, this means they be-come socialized and 'learn the ropes' like a neophyte in any subculture. Basically, the learning of policy is a process by which the recruit discovers and internalizes the rights and obligations of his status and its norms and values. He learns to anticipate what is expected of him so as to win rewards and avoid punishments. Policy is an important element of the newsroom norms.

Now that training and education has become pre-entry, the question of whether socialization actually starts with the recruitment of journalists into colleges and universities and work placements, and through the way they are trained. It is a characteristic of the most high-profile journalism educators in the United Kingdom and United States which they seek to prepare their candidates for jobs on national newspapers and broadcasters such as the BBC, as if working for the so-called leading news providers is the only marker of success. Students are taught to aspire to work at such institutions and to view smaller enterprises, such as local newspapers, niche magazines and alternative media forms, as less worthy. Yet, it is the major mainstream media that have been least successful in sustaining audiences and income and which have been the most precarious employers. This begs the question as to whether journalism schools are capably preparing their students for the reality of media working in the digital age, if they fail to address the bulk of employment opportunities for students.

Journalism does not simply need to have value in 'professional' approaches. Drawing on Zelizer (2004b), Mensing in Franklin and Mensing (2011, p. 20) writes:

> [E]ducators stressing professionalism often focus on a narrow definition of what 'counts' as journalism and who 'counts' as a journalist, widening the disconnect between how journalism is imagined in the academy and how it is actually perceived and practiced 'out there'.

Cokley and Ranke (2011) have advanced suggestions about which model – traditional trade-based apprentice models focused on practice or university-based models leading to graduate entry which focused on theory or a combination of theory and practice – best prepares candidates for the flexible, independent and competitive working environment of journalism. This supposes that the two approaches are mutually exclusive as there is no standard approach to journalism education within the university or the private sector.

Elitism

> The emergence of journalism degrees in the UK is an important structural marker of the occupations slide towards respectability. At the level of the actor, it is hard to imagine a graduate workforce identifying with the traditional posture of the journalist as social outsider.
>
> (Aldridge and Evetts in Tumber, 2003, p. 101)

Submissions to the previous government's Panel on Fair Access to the Professions (2010) showed that more than two-thirds of those entering journalism now come from households where the main wage earner works in a professional or senior managerial occupation. Fewer than 10 per cent of new entrants come from a working-class background, with just 3 per cent from homes headed by semi- or unskilled workers (Dear, 2010). Successive studies have confirmed that growing numbers of top journalists have attended private schools and exclusive universities. Funding cuts in the further education sector have exacerbated the situation, leading to the closure of shorter, more affordable pre-entry training courses and a shift to journalism skills being learnt as part of an undergraduate and postgraduate academic programme. Entry into paid journalism and even into higher education programmes now invariably requires evidence of significant unpaid newsroom experience, which is more feasible to those with conducive geographic and financial backgrounds.

Given that journalism training is, increasingly, funded by students prior to getting jobs, there appears to be little incentive for media organizations to become more accountable and promote socio-economic diversity when they can attract postgraduate entrants on the same salary as school leavers. Similarly, when higher education providers are reliant on increasing student fees and numbers due to cuts in government funding, they are measured on entry profiles, completion rates and graduate employability, all of which point to recruiting, educating and delivering candidates that the industry will want. There are some bursary opportunities available to support training and education in journalism, which vary greatly in the amounts offered and which may still prevent otherwise excellent candidates gaining access to courses.

The independent national Equality Panel was established to examine how inequalities such as gender, age or ethnicity impact on earnings. The study reported that 'deep-seated and systematic differences in economic outcomes remain between social groups'. It found that the situation is compounded over time, so that 'economic advantage and disadvantage reinforce themselves across the lifecycle, and often onto the next generation'. The study called for policy interventions to counteract this widening inequality at each lifecycle stage. Using Free School Meals as a measure of social class, the study reports that by aged 16, male recipients have the lowest average school assessment of any group by gender or ethnicity apart from Gypsy and Traveller children.[3] Geographical context also plays a role in life chances with only 55 per cent of working-age adults employed in the most deprived tenth of areas in England (Department of Communities and Local Government, 2008, updated 2012). Low-income candidates from less urban areas had limited access to work experience opportunities.

The Sutton Trust's 2009 report to the Milburn Commission found that those with an independent schooling – who now constitute 7 per cent of the school-age population – are considerably more likely to take leading jobs in the media (Sutton Trust, 2009). It identified two main implications, first questioning how accessible routes are into certain professions when the type of school attended and the family background appear to be key indicators of success. Second, does the background and experience of senior editorial decision-makers impact on their news judgement and their recruitment strategies? Most of all, it highlighted how undefined the explicit entry profile for journalists is. This study followed their high-profile 2006 investigation into the educational backgrounds of leading journalists, which found that 'opportunities for bright children from non-privileged homes are both nowhere near as good as they should be and have declined in recent decades' (Sutton Trust, 2006). Sir Peter Lampl, Chief Executive, concluded:

> With increasing financial hardship during the early stages of careers, the signs are that the national news media will become even more dominated by those from privileged backgrounds in the future. For a profession that has done much to uncover the inequalities elsewhere in society, this prompts some awkward questions. Is news coverage preoccupied with the issues and interests of the social elite that journalists represent? Should the profession not better reflect the broader social make-up of the audiences it serves?
>
> (Sutton Trust, 2009, p. 2)

In July 2009, the *Guardian*'s Roy Greenslade, a professor of Journalism at the elite graduate centre for journalism education, London's City University, lamented the lack of working-class students on his own programmes (Greenslade, 2009). The discussion continued online over several days and highlighted a host of 'unofficial' industry recruitment criteria, including being related to senior journalists.

Defining journalism, defining journalism education

There are currently very different understandings of the two concepts of journalism and journalism education. To take journalism first, the basic skills of journalism are widely recognized as consisting of newsgathering, news writing and news production, but on the other hand, there is no agreement as to whether journalism is simply a part of the media or a distinct field of its own. This links to the debates over whether its role is that of a public service or predominantly that of a commercial enterprise. The latter view leads to journalism being straightforwardly subsumed into the general media industry, whereas when viewed as a public service, it tends to be defined as a distinct field of its own.

The public-service role of journalism, regarded as that of a necessary support for democratic society, is generally acknowledged even if it is accepted that this role is not static but varies over time and place. It is associated with the claimed traditional values of neutrality, objectivity and fairness. Its commercial role is advocated less, yet is claimed to be a more accurate reflection of how the Press actually operates in today's world (Donsbach, 2004). The traditional public service role is faced with difficult challenges from information and communication technologies, globalization, consumerism and individualism. Added to this, the journalistic standards of objectivity and truth have been called into question by the philosophies of structuralism and post-structuralism.

There is a direct connection between these differing views and the form and structure of journalism education. Certain skills will be common to all programmes, but journalism and media programmes tend to be amalgamated for other components of the curriculum if no distinction is perceived between journalism and other areas of media practice. If the opposite view is held, journalism will be organized and run separately. Where its social, democratic role is emphasized, the commercial function of the Press may be neglected and the curriculum will encompass political and social theories and themes. On the contrary, where the Press is viewed as a business, the curriculum will focus on the commercial side of the industry and devote little attention to aspects associated with its public-service role.

Reflexive model

From a position of 'knowing how' to 'do' journalism, a person can then apply and test out those skills both practically and conceptually until they reach a position of 'being able', so that they personally feel ownership and embodiment of practice. Taking that notion further, it might be said that 'being able' empowers the individual to adapt, shape and subvert that skill or set of skills in accordance with their desired aim. That might for instance enable them to recognize how a feature has been conventionally constructed and so approach it in a tangential way to elicit a whole new set of data or opinions. 'Being able' is also applicable outside the mainstream industry by allowing individuals or groups the ability to use journalism practices as part of their toolkit. One other academic rationale for teaching practice is that its parameters can be tested from a position within practice as well as from the perspective of a consumer of media messages and forms. This is a key argument behind the shift to reflexive research into journalism.

> Rather than reinforce attitudes of the past, journalism educators could work more deliberately to challenge students to reflect critically on the practices and attitudes they encounter during internships and on-the-job training. This reflection could help students stay more flexible and responsive to future change, rather than resistant or indifferent.
>
> (Mensing, 2011, p. 22)

This links into new models of delivery, for example, critical practice, theories of practice, different contextual models.

Journalism educators should look at proposing different models, especially those which rise above notions of industry and mainstream media, that transcend the specificity of preparation for a job.

Conclusion

The significant changes being wrought within and upon the journalism industry today call for a review of the way entrants to the industry are trained and educated. The historic model of preparing journalists to work for mass-circulation print titles and major broadcasters has to be rethought in view of the evidence from around the globe that journalism trainees and graduates have very different and diverse roles in the digital age.

Indeed, the textbooks that students are encouraged to buy differ very little from one another. According to the textbooks, the growing dominance of multimedia and multi-platform journalism, along with interactivity, has had very little impact on the teaching of dominant linear forms of news writing. Assessment is based on students achieving certain 'correct' standards in writing and production that largely cohere with industry practice. Work placements are encouraged in order to reinforce and embed the taught skills. It is in assessment practices that the professional nature of journalism training and education is made most manifest. How well students mirror industry requirements is a key factor in a programme or provider's esteem.

Simultaneously, the very institutions that have shaped and demanded this system and formed the various accrediting bodies that hold power in determining the content and approach of many courses are actually in grave crisis. Their core business is being superseded by non-traditional start-ups. Journalism oriented towards mass audiences, the type of features that are written in one country then syndicated globally, are not as appealing to audiences who are looking for more specific outputs that cater more closely to their circumstances. Readers can differentiate between news-as-product produced unquestioned from press releases and heartfelt journalism generated using creative investigation.

The trainers and educators themselves are often accused of delivering skills and attitudes based on their own previous practitioner careers, rather than encouraging innovative approaches that challenge and reinvigorate conventional ones. For example, a search through the syllabuses of some of the most prestigious establishments shows online journalism being taught either as a separate module or that only certain members of the faculty are labelled as 'online'. This suggests that many educators are not embracing, or are at best pigeonholing, the way that the Internet is a significant driver in the transformation of editorial communication. This begs a series of questions:

1 If, as figures such as decreasing membership of unions and the increase in portfolio working would suggest, journalism is becoming de-professionalized or at least only semi-professional, why do educators and trainers focus on making students 'professional'?
2 Why do so many education or training establishments and accrediting bodies still focus on a top-down hierarchical model of the producer–audience relationship?
3 Why is there still an emphasis on socializing students to work in the mainstream industry, rather than enabling them to be creative, experimental and critical, to inspire new forms of practice? The education of journalists is inextricably tied to workplace needs and expectations; changes in one bring about change in the other.

This chapter has revealed that the current dominant systems for the training and education of journalists throw up issues of elitism, socialization and transfer the training costs from the industry to students. In its wake, this development has heralded accusations of elitism, even within publicly funded bodies such as the BBC. But there are also many opportunities. The expansion in media education in universities offers skills and knowledge previously only accessed by those already within a mainstream journalism career. The acquisition of these skills by a wider audience offers the potential to a new Fifth Estate to work within and alongside the media in areas other than the mainstream. The media industry has the pick of a graduate talent pool given the numbers taking up places on higher education courses. Students receive longer, more in-depth training than they might have received on the job. On good courses, student journalists have the opportunity to become both multiskilled and creative and are encouraged to acquire the habit of lifelong reflection and learning.

To ensure its sustainability, the purpose of higher education training in journalism needs to be debated and configured to secure a clear understanding from educators, students and employers. It has worked in the interests of employers to create a professional ideology of journalism that has at its heart pre-entry graduate training in the model of medicine or law. The major difference between journalism and those professions is that the former does not tend to result in the salaries and lifelong security that medical or legal consultancy can offer to the best qualified. Instead, undergraduate and postgraduate journalism education offers candidates one route onto the bottom rung of a tall ladder as a 'trainee', 'junior' or 'assistant' on the very lowest pay grade and often on short-term contracts. One could be forgiven for thinking that this only serves to heighten the fascination of a career, as so many are still attracted to take out significant loans and debts to enter it despite a lack of stability or long-term rewards.

There is some debate about the purpose and future of journalism and media education. As universities move ever closer to professional training providers, it is now pressing that educators ensure journalism students have the ability to distinguish between journalism as a set of practices and journalists as an occupational group or groups with specific ideologies. Examining these links and tensions can make transparent how an occupational ideology is formed and permit knowing agency on the part of the new entrant.

3 The Journalistic Self

How much do we really know about journalists, when academic and popular knowledge about newsroom activities differs so much? In films and books, for instance, journalists are often cast as crusading heroes righting wrongs and exposing abuses of power. In academic parlance, journalists tend to be judged, often negatively, for their products rather than their actual endeavours. In both cases, the public and scholars rarely get a glimpse of the everyday reality of news production and so it carries a great deal of mystique. This mystique, it appears from the evidence in the previous chapter, serves only to heighten the industry's appeal to young people whose demand for jobs outstrips their availability many times over.

We saw there how journalists learn the skills and knowledge to enter the occupation. But there is a world of difference between knowing 'how to' be a journalist and 'being able' to do the job with confidence and that golden ingredient – professionalism – on a daily basis (Niblock, 2007). New recruits must inevitably undergo a period, if not a lifetime, of acclimatization so as to absorb and adopt the mores and conventions of the field. They need to learn what to do and how to act in order to be a 'proper' journalist.

Very little is actually known about how this happens; few of us ever get to witness the workings of a newsroom and how journalists operate and relate to one another, even less gain insights into how they 'feel' about what they do. As the media are affected by major changes in technology and routines, how do employers and employees maintain a sense of routine, purpose and identity when their roles twist and turn so frequently?

At one time, as we saw in Chapter 2, media practitioners learnt their approach and gained loyalty to their outlet through close mentoring by senior colleagues. There were established career-progression paths, clear job descriptions and editorial hierarchies. Today, the media workplace is characterized by multi-skilling and blurring of roles. Full-time permanent contracts are being replaced by short-term hires creating job

45

uncertainty and fewer fixed affiliations with a news outlet. Yet, the journalistic identity shows no sign of waning. Indeed, some scholars have noted that professional demarcations can feel even stronger when an industry or occupation is under threat. The key question for this chapter is how the notion of professionalization is used within the occupation.

What is professionalism?

> Professional competence is the habitual and judicious use of communication, knowledge, technical skills, clinical reasoning, emotions, values, and reflection in daily practice for the benefit of the individual and community being served.
>
> (Epstein and Hundert, 2002)

The main criteria for professionals include the following:

- Expert and specialized knowledge in the field which one is practicing
- Excellent manual/practical and thinking skills in relation to the profession
- High-quality work
- High standard of professional ethics, behaviour and work activities
- Positive attitude and motivation
- Positive relationships with colleagues.

Most workers aspire to operate professionally. But are the qualities and attributes of media professionalism defined similarly by employers and employees or, indeed, news users? Given the dip in trust in the media, this is an important question which cuts to the core of what a media professional is. According to academics, professionalization can be made manifest in two ways (Nygren, 2011, p. 209):

> It can come from within, when the professionals themselves can exert control over, and form the values and norms for, the profession.
>
> But it can also be used by groups outside the profession, such as owners, state and organizations, to change an occupation and to use it as a system of control and discipline.

The first approach suggests that occupational identity is the biggest influence on professional characteristics, while the second proposes a power-based model. Let us look at each in turn.

Professional identity

The concept of identity can be interpreted in different ways, according to various approaches from psychoanalysis, cultural studies and psychology to name but three. What these various meanings have in common is the idea that identity is not a fixed attribute, but a relational phenomenon. Christiansen et al. (1999) define identity as a composite self, made up of roles and relationships, values, personal desires and goals. Extending this concept to work, he argues that participation in occupations helps to create identity and cement who one is and wishes to become. Kielhofner (2007, p. 106) posits that occupational identity includes a composite of the following:

- One's sense of capacity and effectiveness
- What things one finds interesting and satisfying
- Who one is, as defined by one's roles and relationships
- What one feels obligated to do and believes important
- A sense of the familiar routines of life
- Perceptions of one's environment and what it supports and expects.

According to this view, occupational identity reflects accumulated life experiences that are organized into an understanding of who one has been and a sense of a desired and possible direction for the future. In other words, it fulfils two roles: as a means to defining the self now, and for directing future action.

Another way of looking at identity is drawn from definitions used in social sciences and philosophy. The psychologist Erikson (1968) focused on identity formation in social situations and on the stages people pass through during their lives. He posited that, owing to biological and psychological development, each stage has particular characteristics with regard to how individuals interact with their environment. As such, identity is something that develops gradually rather than being something we are born with. Mead (1934) agrees and relates identity to the concept of self alongside discussions about identity, describing in detail how our sense of who we are is shaped and nuanced through interactions with our environment. According to Mead, self is relational insofar as it can arise only in a social setting where there is social communication. Through communicating with others, we identify with them and adapt our own actions accordingly. Our sense of self can, according to this model, be defined as an organized representation of our theories, attitudes and beliefs about ourselves (McCormick and Pressley, 1997). This is why, to us, our sense of self feels absolutely real and lived, while to someone else it is highly subjective (Purkey, 1970).

Identity development occurs in an inter-subjective field and can be best characterized as an ongoing process, a process of interpreting one-self as a certain kind of person and being recognized as such in a given context (Gee, 2001). In this context, then, identity can also be seen as an answer to the recurrent question: 'Who am I at this moment?'

In the media sphere, occupational identity refers not only to the influence of the conceptions and expectations of other people, including broadly accepted images in society about what a journalist should do, but also to what media practitioners themselves find important in their work and lives based on both their experiences in practice and their personal backgrounds (Tickle, 2000). To what extent both aspects of professional identity are interwoven is unclear but undoubtedly explains why those individuals interviewed pursue a diversity of goals.

Journalistic identity formation might be thought of as a struggle because new journalists have to make sense of varying and sometimes competing perspectives, expectations and roles that they have to confront and adapt to in the digital world.

The varying professional attitudes of different groups of journalists are reflected in the way they perceive their roles. Kepplinger and Kocher (1990) found that whereas British journalists are far more likely to consider themselves as 'entertainers, the voice of the people and politicians by different means' (p. 295) German journalists, by contrast, 'regard themselves more often as critics of negative conditions and situations and as advocates of disadvantaged persons within the population' (p. 295) Both views, of course, correspond with a shared professional view, albeit quite local, and are reinforced through an ethical standpoint.

Social control model

> [O]bviously, journalists are in the end individuals, but news organizations are also sufficiently bureaucratized that very different personalities will act much the same in the same position.
>
> (Gans, 1979, p. 3)

We saw in Chapter 1 that some journalism studies scholars refer to the process of journalistic professionalization as distinctly ideological. An ideology served the interests of media owners and practitioners by distinguishing and promoting a consensus about who is a 'real' journalist and, in the context of blogging and citizen journalism, what should be considered 'real' journalism. In this way, journalistic occupational ideology can be seen as a system of beliefs shared by the whole group.

Schlesinger (1978), for example, writes about news workers' occupational ideology, Golding and Elliott (1979) write of journalism's occupational ideology, while Soloski (1990) talks about an ideology of professionalism. Zelizer (2004b) also mentions journalists' professional ideology. However, most of these authors do not make explicit what this ideology comprises. Schudson describes the occupational ideology of journalism as 'cultural knowledge that constitutes "news judgment", rooted deeply in the communicators' consciousness' (2001, p. 153) with Zelizer (2004a, p. 101) also referring to a collective knowledge that journalists employ. Professional ideology as seen here is a cognitive process, during which the ideas and values of journalists are shaped and other views are rejected (Stevenson, 1995, pp. 37–41; van Ginneken, 1997, p. 73). An example might be the journalism awards system.

Receiving awards and accolades from one's peers is one way that journalists justify their actions and gain prestige and power. Most journalists would say that receiving an award or prize for their work is the ultimate honour and badge of professionalism. However, from another perspective, Johnson (1972) and Allison (1986) suggest that calling yourself a professional is a way to justify an inherent imbalance of power between the professional and the layperson. Take, for instance, the coverage of the UK riots in August 2011, which received criticism from researchers and the communities affected by the unrest. Journalists deflected such criticism by citing the number of awards their coverage had yielded. These were, however, awarded by peers with the same frame of reference rather than by the communities they supposedly serve. So power is maintained by control over the measuring of work performance.

Sociological and occupational analyses of journalists have been fairly rare since the 1970s, when the emphasis shifted to media studies-style analyses of messages and meanings inherent within news output (Glasgow Media Group, 1976, 1980; Philo, 1982). One of the earliest and still influential studies of newsroom power relations is Warren Breed's 'Social Control in the Newsroom' (1955) in which he closely examined how journalists came to adopt and internalize the editorial policies of their organizations. Breed surmised that conformity to newsroom protocols was not realized through managerial coercion but through the realization of strong collegial attachments. Sigelman's (1973) study of TV news supported this by finding journalists would comply with organizational policies to minimize conflict. As discussed in Chapter 1, the creation of clear and rigid routines of news production was an important step in the professionalization of journalism. It also served to create job descriptions and hierarchies of personnel in editorial offices. Tunstall's (1971) study of journalists at work demonstrated adherence to role expectations but also shed light on how journalists conform to standardized patterns of reporting and writing. Gaye Tuchman's work (1972, 1973, 1978) took this idea further by arguing that news routines perform a social, meaning-making function through collaboration with regular sources. In fact, the common thread of most analysis from the 1970s was the 'construction' of news, the idea that it is 'made' rather than 'found' in order to serve dominant forces in society (Altheide, 1976; Schlesinger, 1978; Gans, 1979; Golding and Eliott, 1979; Fishman, 1980). By the 1980s, with the rise to prominence of media studies, research focused more on media messages and media institutions rather than the producers of news themselves. Media organizations, it was felt, placed constraint on their workers, who could only function within tightly delimited parameters (Schlesinger, 1978); Morrison and Tumber, (1988).

More recently, work in the emerging discipline of journalism studies has explored the perceptions of journalists themselves. Bantz (1985) and Ericson et al. (1989) found that journalists do, in fact, contest established working practices and that working relationships and attitudes to authority in the newsroom are rather more complex than previously posited. Many studies in the 1990s and early twenty-first century have adopted an ethnographic or interview approach to reveal practitioner perspectives and details of the news-making process. Among the most notable has been Tumber and Webster's (2006) retelling of the experiences of embedded journalists in the conflict in Iraq, examining relations between the media, the military and government. Cottle's (1993) ethnographical study of British regional television news shed light on how journalists negotiate rigid formats and target audiences to deliver content. In the United States, Eliasoph (1988) and Jacobs (1996) shone light on how local TV stations made news meaningful to engage viewers. Likewise, journalists have published memoirs recalling incidents, judgments and sometimes indiscretions in minute detail (see, for example, Marr, 2004 and Snow, 2004). However useful these accounts are in revealing the workings of an industry usually shrouded from public view, they do not reveal much about newsroom collective behaviour or the impact an organization has on journalists' self-perception and occupational identity. Moreover, they do not account for how journalists gain and retain their sense of professionalism in a changing media world. This is vital given the transformations to working practices wrought by the introduction, sudden in many cases, of new production technologies and routines, coupled with simultaneous cuts in staffing levels in response to challenging market conditions (Franklin, 2003). There have only been limited surveys of the impact these have had on motivation and morale (NUJ, 2007).

News workers have to act 'professionally' so their work can be described as 'journalism', which Ericson et al. (1989) showed comes from them learning a 'vocabulary of precedents' or acquiring an accumulation of shared knowledge. Self-regulation is a marker of autonomy and independence: the idea that only a journalist can judge whether another journalist has performed unethically. There is certainly evidence of a collaboration at the present time against any threat of statutory regulation post-Leveson.[1] Proof of a collective journalistic identity was displayed in 2004 when publication of the Hutton Report prompted public protests by BBC staff against the 'attack on journalism' (Tumber and Palmer, 2004).

But Aldridge and Evetts (2003) maintain that journalists' use of the term professional has corresponded with their declining power and status in the newsroom and is a means to preserve identity. 'In effect, professionals seek to establish a monopoly on expertise that makes them irreplaceable, giving them the ability to control entry to their ranks (Singer, 2003, p. 141). But can terms such as 'reporting' and 'writing' be defined as core knowledge in the same way that medical professionals might have core knowledge of the human circulatory system? Surely reporting and writing are skills, albeit crucial to the craft, but easily shaped and nuanced according to the context in which they are being performed?

It is also not essential that journalists have graduate or postgraduate qualifications to enter the industry, though the vast majority do. What counts are organizational expectations of behaviour and performance standards and this is where control takes place. It is especially important, as a consequence, that universities and colleges make these forces transparent so that students can be mindful of them and forge their own values and identities as ethical journalists prior to entering the field.

Soloski (1989) looks at the way that news organizations use professionalization as a means to develop rules – news policies that in turn control the behaviour of journalists. This is because newsrooms have to work quickly and there is no time for lengthy discussions or dealing with dissent – all involved must agree. The nature of journalistic efficiency requires editorial staff to work fairly autonomously yet as part of a team. The fast-paced nature of news means it is virtually impossible for the senior editor of a major news outlet to carefully monitor the practices and behaviours of individual staff members or sections. Rules and regulations can control and restrain behaviour but are also difficult to enforce in such a fluid environment and might not encourage good working relations in creative teams.

> The norms of behaviour that emanate from news professionalism constitute a *trans*-organisational control mechanism. Since the behaviour of journalists is rooted – to a great extent – in shared professional norms, the minimizes the problem of how news organizations are able to maintain control over journalists.
>
> (Soloski, cited in Tumber and Prentoulis 2005, p. 57)

How is professionalism maintained?

Journalists are at the nexus of these two sides of professionalism – the demands of the organization – standards, routines, company goals – and the occupational values and identity they develop themselves (Örnebring, 2008b). But how does this work in practice and is there an equal balance between the two? Furthermore, can the two sides be seen as mutually exclusive or even compatible, especially in the context of greater competition, corporatization and convergence?

> The professional demands following the market logic are stronger than ever, and a weaker professionalisation 'from within' could make it more difficult to keep these kinds of professional standards high.
>
> (Nygren, 2011, p. 219)

The ideology may be made manifest by a number of themes including editorial values, news-reporting strategies and formal codes agreed upon and shared by members of the occupational group. This is deemed ideology because it is the dominant way in which news people validate and give meaning to their work. Journalism's ideology has, for example, been analysed as a 'strategic ritual' to position oneself in the profession (Tuchman, 1972). When faced with public criticism, such as over the phone-hacking complaints in the United Kingdom, journalists applied ideological values to defend the need for popular journalism and autonomous practice free from external statutory intervention.[2] According to former newspaper editor and BBC correspondent Andrew Marr, 'regular doses of hype, sloppy reporting and uncorrected mistakes' (Marr, 2004, p. xv) are parts of the price of the freedom of the Press.

If this view is as widespread among journalists as this writer implies, then there is still much fertile sociological territory to be charted in their work. Where the boundaries of acceptable and competent practice lie, how these vary within and between media, and how practitioners learn to work within these are surely areas requiring urgent attention. Mistakes occur in every sphere of employment, but journalists' mistakes are of particular interest because of their role in the distribution of knowledge (Dickinson, 2007).

Such is the sense of authenticity and justification that research by Russo (1998) suggests that journalists identify themselves more easily with the profession of journalism than, for example, with the medium or media company that employs them. Golding and Elliott (1979), Merritt (1995) and Kovach and Rosenstiel (2001) describe these as

- Public service: journalists provide a public service (as watchdogs or 'news hounds', active collectors and disseminators of information);
- Objectivity: journalists are impartial, neutral, objective, fair and (thus) credible;
- Autonomy: journalists must be autonomous, free and independent in their work;
- Immediacy: journalists have a sense of immediacy, actuality and speed (inherent in the concept of 'news');
- Ethics: journalists have a sense of ethics, validity and legitimacy.

(cited in Deuze, 2005b, p. 447)

Production context and the impact on output

The emerging use of 'content' instead of 'news' or 'journalism' to describe material published, posted or broadcast suggests that journalists' work is little more than 'stuff', filling a designated space, rather than the carefully crafted result of quality reporting. Intrusion, dumbing down and 'infotainment' are some of the factors that have led to calls for the industry to be more open. One result has been an increasing disconnection between the public and journalism, evident in the declining reputation of the journalist in opinion polls and in popular culture. Think how journalists were once portrayed in the cinema. From the wise-cracking Hildy (Rosalind Russell) in *His Girl Friday* (1940) to Clark Kent (Christopher Reeve) and Lois Lane (Margot Kidder) in *Superman* (1978). Celluloid journalists were crusading public servants, working for the good of society. Today, the public has withdrawn its affection, with film lampooning the seemingly vacuous, image-obsessed nature of the corporate, professional, self-seeking journalist, epitomized by Courtney Cox's Gale Weathers in the *Scream* trilogy (1996, 1997 and 2000). Maintaining the public's faith in journalism as a watchdog for democracy, rather than as entertainment, is vital. The physical and systematic organization of newsrooms impacts directly on the scope of journalists' work through the layout of the space, the structuring of the editing process and the demarcations between different roles. Journalists trained on a locally owned newspaper spend a lot of time out and about knocking on doors, looking for the extraordinary in the ordinary and reflecting a community through pages and pages of stories. Editors did not like to see staff spending too much time languishing at their desks. Then large conglomerates with an eye on 'efficiency savings' bought up these titles and transformed working practices. Reporters would arrive at work one morning to find themselves in a swish new carpeted office, but with fewer staff members and even fewer pages to fill. Despite the cheaper production costs of on-screen page make-up, owners reduced the number of local district pages and increase the advertising. Now reporters talk of not leaving the office much, dealing via email or telephone with press officers. Journalists in these new streamlined operations had the tools to make their job quicker and easier – the technology was not at fault, rather it was the profiteering of owners that was wholly out of step with the communities they were meant to serve. So mass communication became more top-down: a 'few' mediating to the 'many'.

Editing systems can also erode the autonomy of the reporter in practice. Content-management systems enable senior editors to observe, direct and alter a story while it is being produced. For example, a study of Bloomberg News by Machin and Niblock (2010) described how editors in different continents could make suggestions about how a story would be adapted for a particular audience. Again, this contrasts with the mythology of the autonomous voice of the reporter.

Kepplinger and Kocher carried out a comparative analysis of copy flow systems in editorial offices around the globe and noted that the United States and United Kingdom have some of the strictest divisions between different roles:

> In West Germany, however, there is – apart from a few exceptions – no distinct separation between the tasks of reporter and sub-editor. There is also no distinct separation between these two and he writers of articles expressing opinion.
>
> (1990, p. 292)

Where there are more roles working in closer co-operation, they say, the greater the orientation towards professional expectations and, in turn, the stronger the influence of professional standards. As such, editorial structures probably have a significant impact on the final output. This was borne out by research into newsroom processes in a commercial radio news agency in the United Kingdom, Independent Radio News, where a news desk assistant confirmed 'process drives content' (Machin and Niblock, 2008).

Career routes

A professional framework works well for journalists as it rewards and recognizes good behaviour. One the one hand, this is good for employers seeking to preserve the status quo and exert control over staffs. On the other hand, it can be dangerous if journalists seek their rewards from their peers' esteem rather than their companies. By providing opportunities for editorial advancement, such as elevation to chief reporter, news organizations are able to reward individuals with the illusion that they have more power, yet they are given more access to the real hierarchy of power than they had before, such as decision-making over allocation of resources. This maintains goodwill and has secured a general professional attitude that it is better not to become management but to be seen as an autonomous reporter, albeit with no control over resources or the means to report.

The editorial meeting

One news editor, interviewed for this book, described in detail how the three editorial meetings per day worked to ensure adherence to newsroom policy:

> Every member of my team knows that I absolutely hate having to put out corrections and I hope they share my professional embarrassment at having made a mistake that has to be very publicly put right. For me there is no worse feeling in a newsroom – apart from being beaten to a story. So having that common value, that common and total respect for the facts has to be at the absolute core of journalistic professionalism. If a mistake were made and a correction has to go out I would certainly be making my feelings very plain to the individual involved because a professional mechanism has broken down

at that point – the mechanism of checking. And that shouldn't be down to one person.

Editorial meetings – morning, lunch and evening in a twenty-four-hour rolling newsroom – are absolutely at the core of helping to build team professionalism. The enthusiasm and faith in the team of the news editor should be infectious and inspiring. It is about letting the team know 'this is not a game it is a service and one that should be taken damn seriously', that a product is being supplied and it should be as good as it can be. If rivals outstrip us in providing news on the agenda that way I am going to want to know why we aren't pushing as hard as other newsrooms. Sometimes it's resources of course, but other newsrooms are also down to a pretty small core of journalists working on key stories. So most national newsrooms share the chance to shine if they think hard enough and smart enough. Any national newsroom worth its salt should be scoring points frequently.

The editorial meeting sets the tone of delivering content as fast as possible and as good as it can be. Editors can also set realistic but demanding targets of the team. At the next editorial meeting, there's a chance to debrief on why it didn't happen as well as it might but also to praise team members and celebrate as a team. It is really important to recognise achievement.

When asked how staff are disciplined, the editor said:

Public dressing downs might work in some newsrooms that operate on a culture of fear but I don't think you get the most out of people that way. There are signals you can put out to let individuals know you aren't happy – after a meeting I could ask them for a second – 'I need a word'. If I ask for a minute, they know it is more serious. If I ask if they have got five minutes they know it is really serious. It becomes like a shorthand for that.

The induction of new staff

One editor, interviewed for this book, described how induction is a gradual process of inculcation into newsroom norms rather than overt instruction. Gradually, new staffers are given greater and greater responsibility as they 'earn' trust.

In a national newsroom, no-one walks through the door without us knowing they are good. We will have checked them out thoroughly first and usually their reputation would precede them. For example, good reporters in regional news would be the people who file regularly to us. We would know the quality of their writing and be aware of their abilities as a reporter. You watch them and I can remember saying on a number of occasions to new people when they've asked for feedback on their progress – 'if no-one is taking you to one side then you know you are doing ok'. But you would not let a new staffer or freelancer have free rein to produce work for whatever platform without the closest of checking. They would gradually be given bigger stories as trust was earned. But new members of staff have to expect to have their work picked over. They may not like it but that is just tough in the early days of life in a new newsroom. No-one will trust you until you have proven yourself.

Your workers have to care about their standards and the team around them needs to be working as hard as it can together to get things right.

Solomon (1970) examined the way individuals in various occupations balance roles in different organizations and as organizations change with self-conceptions formed at earlier stages in their careers. One of his conclusions was that an employee's occupational commitment and their self-conception are linked in a number of ways: where the linkage is weak the employee experiences difficulties. In an era of increasing casualization of media work, the study of how media organizations nurture adherence to workplace norms and routines should be a source of particular interest for contemporary media sociology.

Spaces for autonomous practice?

A major criticism levelled at prescriptive theories of journalism is that they do not account for the diversity of practices and motivations in newsrooms. For instance, van Zoonen (1998) identifies a need for accounts that reflect 'moments of agency and subjectivity in journalism and which incorporate(s) the diversity in the field' (p. 71). Journalists are not one big homogenous group, and journalistic organizations vary hugely in terms of their location, their audience and their purpose. With most research centred on mainstream, national output, we know little about the practices and attitudes of the other 99 per cent of journalists.

For instance, journalists might adopt their organizational identities quite actively; a political reporter and a columnist might negotiate their organization identity subjectively in different ways. Aldridge and Evetts (2003) say that journalists and employers have embraced the discourse of professionalism and use it as a form of self-discipline, which has eased the imposition of radical changes to the organization of work. One major transformation to the culture of journalism as non-professional journalists threaten occupational boundaries is that more journalists aspire to an image of professional respectability rather than operating on its margins. McManus (1994, p. 203) writes: 'A reporter or editor in a profit-maximising media firm who subordinates market standards to those of journalism may be tolerated as long as a counter clerk at McDonald's who refused to sell fried food.' Professional identity serves as a marker of cultural value. Professionalism gives meaning to the work at a time when its value is under significant threat, fostering self-belief and respect. Labour ceases to become simply work but rather something a journalist would do over long hours – as long as it takes to do good work.

Journalists are social actors who sometimes display 'delinquent' behaviour that breaches ethical, legal and professional codes. This delinquency is usually blamed on a breakdown in newsroom management, but perhaps attention also needs to be paid to how individual journalists come to be part of the social bond of the newsroom that helps to differentiate between correct and incorrect behaviour. Or does professionalization dissolve those social bonds and replace them with competitive zeal?

Predating the phone-hacking revelations by several years, Dickinson (2007) examines the sociology of crime to shed light on how deviant behaviour can become socially acceptable in newsrooms, and how under certain pressured conditions there can be a shift in collective identity about what constitutes acceptable behaviour.

Foucault's (1979) description of the process of 'normalization' explains how identities are formed and maintained. Normalization refers to the social processes through which ideas and actions come to be seen as 'natural' and 'normal'. In *Discipline and Punish*, Foucault describes how individuals are rewarded or punished symbolically in certain settings for conforming to or conflicting with accepted behaviour. His argument is that discipline creates 'docile bodies', capable of functioning unquestioningly in orderly ways.

While it may seem far fetched for journalists to think of themselves as symbolically coerced into certain actions, the notion of self-discipline is firmly embedded in the occupation. The evidence for this might be how the BBC insists on every staff member undergoing training in the midst of a crisis. Another form of discipline comes through occupational identity, say Aldridge and Evetts (2003):

> [A]n occupational identity gives individuals a sense of self and strongly influences and affects occupational and indeed other behaviours. The community of fellow workers and the hierarchies of positions in organizations and other work places (such as peers, superiors and juniors) constantly reiterate and reinforce this sense of self and position as well as appropriate behaviours and work decisions and choices (p. 97).

They cite the example of how radical changes to the journalism sector have gone through with minimal objection. While there have been strikes over job cuts, many of the alterations to practices and systems and cuts have been absorbed by vocationally oriented staff committed to delivering an excellent product. While they might not see journalism as a profession per se, they certainly see themselves as professional.

Competitor-colleagues

Competition is assumed to be a motivating force that pushes all players to do their best. Newsrooms often rely on internal rivalry to provoke employees' efforts and spur creativity. There is often internal competition to get the lead story, for instance, or to be allocated the star interview by the editor. Tunstall (1971) takes the view that one important way in which the newsroom agenda tends to be set is by the social and hierarchical relationship between journalists; he writes about 'competitor-colleague' relationships, and of 'newsgathering for newsgatherers'. He describes a world in which decisions are made by reference to a perception of colleagues' esteem. The journalist's source of rewards is located not among the readers, who are manifestly their clients, but among their colleagues and superiors. Instead of adhering to societal and professional ideals, the journalist redefines their values to the level of the newsroom group. The journalist thereby gains not only status reward but also acceptance in a solidarity group engaged in interesting, varied and sometimes important work (Breed, in Tumber 1999, p. 84).

Behind such rewards are realities of proprietorial controls 'exercised, as in any other capitalistic organization, through the appointment of likeminded personnel in key management positions who are delegated to carry out boss's will' (McNair, 1998, p. 107). Not only is the competition between news organizations and between journalists defined as necessary and useful, but defining it as such creates the expectation that news workers will seek to do better than their 'competitor-colleague and their organizations' (Bantz, in Tumber, 1999, p. 139).

The danger is that this stamps out all conflict, creativity or innovation by categorizing employees into winners and losers based solely on senior editors' own preconceptions. A more collaborative, collegial approach might work in the best interests of the newsroom's capacity to innovate and succeed.

Marrying personal and professional values

What happens when journalists' own personal desires are in conflict with the changing professional landscape? In the dynamic media context, do the changes to day-to-day working, the pressures, tighter deadlines, tougher competition, conflict with what journalists personally desire and experience as 'good'? Might any conflict lead to friction in journalists' occupational identity in cases in which the 'personal' and the 'professional' are too far removed from each other? The NUJ is campaigning for a conscience clause to be brought into journalists' staff contracts to permit them to dispute unethical demands without fear of punitive action.

So far we have little data on journalists themselves and their responses to the overarching mechanisms of control that Foucault (1979) suggests are in place. To understand this better, we need data on the features of contemporary media work that cohere into a sense of what it means to act as a 'professional journalist'. Thus, while much has been written on the indirect control of journalistic activity (McQuail, 1992, 2003) we also need to attend to the direct control operating within professional groups of journalists in specific settings. Professional identity is not a stable entity; it cannot be interpreted as fixed or unitary (Coldron and Smith, 1999). It is a complex and dynamic equilibrium where professional self-image is balanced with a variety of roles journalists feel that they have to play.

Historical, sociological, psychological and cultural factors may all influence the journalist's sense of self as a reporter or editor. Furthermore, professional identity may consist of many sub-identities that may conflict or align with each other (Mishler, 1999). According to Mishler, it is better to recognize in the definition of identity that a plurality of sub-identities exists. Mishler (1999, p. 8) uses the metaphor of 'our selves as a chorus of voices, not just as the tenor or soprano soloist'. Gee and Crawford (1998) believe that we can take on different identities, depending upon the social setting, yet there are relationships between these identities. Continuing the metaphor, it can be concluded that the better the relationships between the different identities, the better the chorus of voices sounds.

Conclusion

Professional identity is an ongoing process of interpretation and re-interpretation of experiences (Kerby, 1991), a notion that corresponds with the idea that the occupational development of a journalist never stops and can be best seen as a process of lifelong learning. Professional identity formation is not only an answer to the question: 'What type of journalist am I at this moment?', but also an answer to the question: 'What type of journalist do I want to become?' Journalists engage in critical reflection to evaluate not only their future editorial decision-making but also link it to notions about what being a journalist is and where they want to be in the future. If professional journalistic identity is an ongoing process, this means that it is dynamic, not stable or fixed.

This is useful as it implies both the person and the context. A journalist's professional identity is not entirely unique. Media workers are expected to behave professionally, but not simply by adopting professional characteristics, including proscribed knowledge and attitudes. Journalists differ in the way they adhere to these characteristics depending on the value they personally attach to them. A journalist may to some extent develop his or her own culture.

A journalist's professional identity may also consist of sub-identities, based on the different contexts in which they work – such as different beats or different employment arrangements. Some of these sub-identities may be broadly linked and can be seen as the core of journalists' professional identity, such as 'reporter', while others may be more peripheral, such as 'uploader'.

Ideally, these sub-identities do not conflict. During initial training or education, student journalists often experience conflict in trying to balance their personal values with the occupation demands of the competitive, pressurized newsroom environment. Experienced journalists may also experience inner conflict as evidenced in the NUJ study when new technology was introduced and practices altered.

Agency is an important element of professional identity. This means that journalists have to be active in the process of professional development. There are various ways in which journalists can exercise agency, depending on the goals they pursue and the resources they utilize to reach their goals. In addition, it can be argued that professional identity is not something journalists have per se, but something they use in order to make sense of themselves as journalists. The way they explain and justify things in relation to other people and contexts expresses, as it were, their professional identity.

Journalism is facing a barrage of criticism from governments, audiences and now from within its own industry. How do we start to understand the breakdown in professionalism so apparent in the actions of certain individuals and groups of journalists? Journalists are facing immense pressures due to increased competition and the need to work across several platforms simultaneously. Furthermore, work contracts have become more tenuous with ever-greater job uncertainty. In this changing climate, there is an urgent need for a deeper understanding of journalists' motivations, how they shape what they do at work and how they do it. Research in media studies and journalism studies has tended to focus on the products of journalists and to some extent on their practices, but there has been little research into the identity of journalists themselves. The evolving practices and contexts for journalism demand a closer look at how the occupation defines and regulates itself. While some areas of the industry react with opprobrium when things go awry, there seems to be a view within journalism itself that the rough inevitably comes with the smooth, as Andrew Marr put it. This is fascinating as it highlights some uncharted areas such as where journalists think the boundaries lie between professional and unprofessional behaviour, and how journalists learn to navigate and negotiate these practices.

Some media analysts are casting doubt on the benefits of professionalism, fearing that standardization could stifle diversity and creativity with the net effect of halting progress (Glasser, 1992). One important issue is the way that professionalization poses a challenge of individual journalistic autonomy – one that this book argues is the biggest threat to journalism standards and ethics. If the individual ideals of journalism practitioners are subordinated to those of a group or organization, then journalism loses the passion and zeal that gives it momentum.

In response, those seeking to define a journalist have been forced to investigate what the person does rather than what environment they work in or what their employment contract states. While unresolved, the emerging consensus would seem to be that a journalist is someone who adheres to the ethos that the professional has sought to establish – fairness, accuracy, public service – regardless of their medium, and despite the fact that a number of accredited, employed 'professionals' overtly flout these principles. What matters is not the practitioner's context so much but the nature of their activity.

4 Media Accountability

In the professions, when a practitioner, such as a top physician, commits a blunder, the consequences are plain to see. The cause and effect of that negative act will be scrutinized by the physician's peers and regulatory bodies and, chances are, they will not be allowed to practise again. But in the media, the causal links between misreporting and negative consequences on individuals and society are much harder to prove.

As mentioned at the outset, countless 'traditional' journalists seeing their audiences migrate to these alternative 'unofficial' sources of information bemoan the fact that blogs and user-generated sites do not abide by ethical practices and principles such as accuracy and objectivity. These concerns have two roots: first, there is the fear of losing revenue from subscriptions or advertising if audience figures drop as audiences migrate to free content. Second, the mainstream fears losing journalistic authority. The second fear taps directly into the idea covered at the start of this book – that journalists struggle with the idea of any threat to their distinctive status as professionals.

Legal rulings have already set a precedent for this; courts have determined that bloggers, filmmakers and other practitioners may qualify as journalists. For example, in 2006 in O'Grady v. Superior Court of Santa Clara County, the court stated that it is not its place to distinguish the professional status of the practitioner as this would

> imperil a fundamental purpose of the First Amendment, which is to identify the best, most important, and most valuable ideas not by and sociological or economic formula, rule of law, or process of government, but through the rough and tumble competition of the memetic marketplace.[1]

Ethical values have frequently been cited as what distinguishes a professional journalist from an amateur, a passion for truth seeking (Wasserman cited in Thomas, 2005, p. 16). Though given recent high-profile breaches of moral and legal codes that distinction is wearing a bit thin. How is it that 'good' journalists behave illegally and unethically within a professionalized media? If journalists now operate in a more rigorous, stringent context, as outlined in the previous chapters, surely that should mean a rise in ethics and standards? Given that journalists today are expected to be better educated, to have undertaken a higher level of pre-entry training, and then go onto work in newsrooms with established routines and structures of command, you could be mistaken for thinking that lapses in conduct would be few and far between. Yet, at the time of writing, the UK print media have been scrutinized by the Leveson Inquiry following allegations of routine hacking of mobile phones. In the United States, there have been scandals surrounding the fabrication of sources and even whole stories, among other things. So it is questionable whether the shift to professionalization within the mainstream sector has been a help or a hindrance to media accountability.

In the digital age, who a journalist is accountable to is a key question which cuts to the very core of trust and public service. Throughout history, the media have fought vigorously to protect their autonomy and freedom from overarching state control. While subject to some state and self-regulation, the media are for the most part independent. Recent scandals, such as the *News of the World* phone-tapping revelations and the BBC *Newsnight* affair, have led to public outcries for tighter curbs. Measuring unethical reporting and its impact on consumers of journalism is complex. The PCC, for instance, only accepts complaints under strict conditions so its figures of 7,341 complaints during 2011 is certainly just the tip of the iceberg. The *Guardian*'s readers' editor, who investigates concerns about reporting on that title, received more than 45,000 calls, letters and emails during the first six years of this new position and currently receives around 10,000 enquiries a year.

The watchdog and support group MediaWise suggests that many of the people worst affected by poor journalistic practice do not, or cannot, complain, owing to factors such as the language barrier or the time constraints and the requisite know-how.[2] For example, the PCC will not accept third-party complaints. The impact of misreporting can be great. It has been established, for example, that insensitive reporting of suicides can contribute to other individuals taking their own lives.[3] This begs the question of whether it is non-professional media practitioners that are threatening abiding journalism principles and standards.

Some, such as Hallin (1997), take the view that professionalizing journalism through formal training and education can in fact protect journalists individually and collectively from creeping commercial and political pressures. This is why, despite these sometimes devastating ethical lapses, in keeping with other professions, journalists on both sides of the Atlantic fiercely protect their autonomy and independence. As we have seen, freedom from interference, whether by proprietors, business interests, politicians or the state, is a robustly defended principle by a media keen to be seen as a watchdog for democracy, so much so that the mainstream media have used this to defend their reputation against the perceived encroachment of bloggers and citizen journalists. Anyone without professional credentials, say many in the industry, cannot be trusted. Among the most powerful and persuasive critics is David Leigh, the respected investigative journalist, who said: 'We're not talking about "unmediated media" here. We're talking about corrupted media. And the on-line world, with it's don't pay, something-for-nothing mentality, is very vulnerable to lies and propaganda' (Leigh, 2007).

But can we only blame Internet interlopers for these incursions? While the public have always expressed concerns about journalists going 'too far', today they are no longer willing to accept the motives or expertise of many of the major news brands. Few people trust the tabloid press, ranking them below the politicians or other figures they seek to expose.[4] As a result, the mainstream and its citizen counterparts are considering their responses in order to rebuild faith in public communication.

Some schools of thought believe the way forward is to implement tighter regulation and statutory controls over media practices, in order to bring the media more in line with other professions. But it might equally be argued that professionalization has, in fact, been a hindrance to improving standards. Real and lasting changes might be better wrought from within the industry and at the very grass roots of how societies perceive the role and function of journalism.

To whom are journalists accountable?

A fundamental place to begin any discussion around accountability is to reflect on who journalists are responsible to. It is no easy question for any paid reporter to answer and opinions vary. Typically, we might think of the following groups as being the main recipients or beneficiaries of journalists' work:

1 Their audiences
2 The public interest
3 Fellow journalists
4 Employers

In the first instance, journalists have a remit to deliver content that meets their audience's expectations. If they do not meet demand, viewers, listeners, readers and surfers will turn away from the outlet. As such, there is a drive for consistency in tone and in editorial judgement over the selection of stories, angles, pictures and vocabulary. The choice of sources will also tend to reflect the priorities of the readers the outlet is seeking to target in order to engage them. As all news outlets publish to the Web, they are ploughing resources and know-how into interactively so as to build communities of news consumers. Newsrooms wish to be seen as in conversation with their audiences, not merely delivering content in a one-way route.

But audience expectations and audience needs are different things. Most journalists and indeed news organizations would say that their primary responsibility is to serve the public interest. Gans' (1980, pp. 234–5) study discovered that journalists see themselves as professionals working for a predominantly lay clientele, the audience, who the journalists give what they need rather than what it wants. For example, the BBC College of Training states on its website:

> Being a journalist in any news organisation carries with it a responsibility to the public – both to your audiences and to the public more broadly.

> Journalism that isn't accountable to the public is no more than entertainment.[5]

This is little different from what the US-based National Association of Citizen Journalists says about its approach:

> NACJ membership and training empowers citizen journalists for the exciting task of discovering, writing and reporting news with a level of professionalism that was once the standard in major media outlets.[6]

Journalists are also encouraged to be accountable to their fellow professionals. By upholding high standards, especially levels of accuracy, journalists are ideally meant to preserve the occupation's status in the eyes of the public and officialdom so as to remain a credible watchdog for democracy. Sloppy grammar, failure to check facts and a tendency to break ethical and legal codes has a knock-on effect on all journalists, not just the perpetrator. This has been proven to be the case in the UK local media in the wake of phone hacking by national journalists. Senior newsroom personnel told the 2011 Society of Editors conference that regular sources and even official bodies such as the police were now reluctant or resistant interviewees over fears that journalists of any sort cannot be trusted.[7]

Accountability to employers operates at the fundamental level of professional propriety in terms of adhering to a contract. But a journalist is also accountable to the symbolic role of the media as the Fourth Estate, resisting any influence from outsiders. Gans' (ibid.) study also noted that 'The primary supplier of journalistic feedback is, of course, the person (or persons) who hold power over the journalists' (ibid. p. 235). Crucially, when he asked journalists 'for whom they were writing, producing, or editing, they always began with their superiors, and some went no further' (op. cit.). This suggests that in an era of greater pressures on journalists, one in which professionalism is defined by a strict adherence to the deadlines, routines and norms of the commercial newsroom, practitioners may lose sight of the wider implications of accountability.

How ethics and standards are managed within the industry

Historically, journalists have tended to outwardly resist any form of influence or regulation from outside the occupation. As such, media institutions are generally externally controlled at only the broadest, organizational level. The conditions for their operation are typically the subject of regulation designed to safeguard independence from political interference, prevent unfair competition in the marketplace, protect individual rights and public interests, and so on, but the control of their daily operations and the behaviour of their employees largely remains in their own hands.

There are two main internal ways in which newsrooms manage and seek to maintain ethical standards: self-regulation and through the promotion of objectivity.

Self-regulation

In an age of mounting pressures through competition, speed and influence from external sources, one of the main ways in which the professionalized journalistic media are reminded to stay attuned to ethics and standards is through adherence to professional and regulatory codes. In any profession, its members are expected to avoid abusing the power imbalance between the professional and the client by look-ing after their client's best interests. Often, professions will seek to earn the trust of their clients by adopting agreed professional codes of con-duct that make clear their minimum of ethical and behavioural conduct. In this way, they make themselves answerable or accountable to oth-ers they work with in the course of duty. Over the development of journalism as a professionalized occupation, a number of bodies have created codes of behaviour and ethical standing that they assert should be applied to all journalists. These bodies include the Society for Pro-fessional Journalists in the United States and, in the United Kingdom, the National Union of Journalists, Press Complaints Commission and the Society of Editors. The US-based Society for Professional Journal-ists code's basic principles – seek truth and report it; minimize harm; act independently; be accountable – remain the heart of good journal-ism ethics. But the explanations following those principles are rooted in an age of print and television. SPJ's website explains that the soci-ety borrowed the code of the American Society of Newspaper Editors in 1926. SPJ developed its own code in 1973 and revised it in 1984, 1987 and most recently in 1996, when digital journalism was in its infancy. It is odd that the longest gap between revisions since SPJ wrote its own code would come during a time of such profound change for journalism. Within these groups generally there may also be subsets for specialism, such as codes relating to photojournalism.

A major function of modern regulation is to empower the public by giving them the ability to check and verify that someone who claims to do a particular job is actually authorized to do so. For trades this is often through an approved identity card, renewed every few years on completion of the revised exams. For professions this takes the form of published lists of approved professionals. Websites have then developed to help find a recognized professional who is either local or has specialist knowledge relevant to the searcher's needs. Sometimes the regulators publish these lists freely. There are already some who want to see an approved list of journalists, such as *Daily Mail* editor Paul Dacre.[8] The public also want to be able to complain and to have bad journalists removed from the register.

Objectivity and its limits

Ethics and norms exist in the workplace for a host of purposes, some ritualistic. They provide unity to specific groups and can help to distin-guish one occupation from another. One of these norms is objectivity.

Rules about objectivity have become enshrined in journalism codes of conduct, and are said to serve as the main marker that distinguishes the 'professional' reporter from the untrained amateur. It resounds particularly in US and UK newsrooms, where there is an understanding that journalists will be seen to report the facts truthfully and without personal bias. From an occupational standpoint, the reinforcement of an expectation of objectivity, especially when conceived of as ensuring public service, might be seen as a way for news organizations to maintain quality and standards.

Objectivity is a cardinal principle of journalism, which denotes that journalists should be impartial in their reporting. Yet there has been a longstanding debate, which continues, on whether journalists can or should be objective. When the very meaning of the term is contested among journalists, academics and commentators, it is even more difficult to unpack its relevance to media working in the digital age. Nonetheless, understanding its emergence offers a key to understanding the development of a professionalized media. It becomes evident how objectivity is not a fixed concept or journalistic mantra at all, but a dynamic notion applied to varying degrees at different moments.

Media historians, such as Schudson (1978) and Kaplan (2002) have identified objectivity and truth-seeking as an ideological endpoint in the journey towards professionalism. This makes sense when we consider how mainstream journalists tend to use the concept of objectivity to distinguish their occupation and the value of its practitioners from encroaching cyber citizen hacks.

The notion of objectivity is actually a relatively recent development in journalism. Until the early part of the twentieth century, reporting tended to be highly opinionated and partisan. Horace Greeley's New York *Tribune*, one of the leading American journals of the mid nineteenth century, campaigned against slavery, warned against creeping imperialism and called for universal welfare. Indeed, one of his leading correspondents was the German scholar Karl Marx. The *Tribune* and its mission chimed with the times and sought to make sense of the rapid transformations facing the emerging super power and its citizens. While partisan journalism is generally viewed with disdain by the professionalized media, nations around the globe with non-neutral journalism can have more passionate political cultures. As Nichols and McChesney (2005) note about the United States the 1820s and 1830s was a high-point for partisan journalism, characterised by broad democratic participation among those who were allowed to vote.[9] However, partisan media systems also have their distinct disadvantages, not least evidenced by the propaganda and lies of the Press in Nazi Germany as a means to symbolically disenfranchise its citizens and repress free thought.

Since the 1970s, sociologists have challenged objectivity's ability to effect what its practitioners claim:

> Bringing to the forefront issues like values, roles and ethics, what emerged from (the sociological) literature was a growing recognition that journalists crafted standards of action collectively with others and that those standards in turn structured journalists' approaches to news.
>
> (Zelizer, 2004b, p. 58)

In the same vein, Tuchman (1972), Tumber and Prentoulis (2005) and others have suggested objectivity is in itself illusory and an unstable basis for reporting. One version of the critique is based the nature of language itself, Saussure, Barthes and a host of successors have emphasized that language is never a pure, neutral denotative representation of a world 'out there' (Barthes, 2009). According to Taylor (1985) language constitutes rather than merely describes. Articulation is a human process, both individual and sociocultural whereby a journalist, however intent they might be on avoiding descriptive adverbs and adjectives, can never be neutral by virtue of the fact they are human. News language is by its very essence a mediation of a truth, an interpretation, but not an objective account. Herein lies one of the main tensions in promoting journalistic objectivity and autonomy as 'professional', as Borden and Bowers point out:

> [I]f knowledge is contingent rather than pre-existent, epistemologically constructed rather than objective, constituted rather than depicted by language, professionalism arguably functions as an impediment to media morality by occluding the journalist's role in creating news. Scraps of information replace the holistic cloth of knowledge.
>
> (2008, p. 358)

Threats to media accountability from within

Journalists all over the world voice concerns regarding their freedom to work as they please. Editorial autonomy is invoked in the face of any extra-journalistic or management-driven force. In an increasingly transparent and sometimes even participatory news ecology, 'autonomy' as an individual-level concept is quite problematic. There are four main challenges that make any attempt at professional autonomy and accountability very difficult, mainly stemming from attempts to manage ethical behaviour on an organizational basis:

- Relationships with sources
- Conformity to norms and routines of news
- Ownership
- Social control.

Relationship with sources

At one time, when journalism was less professionalized and at the lower levels certainly occupied by members of more diverse social groups, power brokers and journalists came from quite distinct perspectives. Their coexistence was relatively unproblematic given their clearly defined roles. Yet the growing professonalization of the media, coupled with the increasingly privileged backgrounds of its operators, tends to muddy the waters.

In parliamentary democracies, such as the United Kingdom, there is a close occupational cross over between decision-makers and powerful social groups. The mutually interdependent relationship between politicians and journalists has come in for particular scrutiny. Each side relies on the other for its living and purpose to a major degree. In post-industrial Western societies, particularly where there is so much ease of access to digital media, the production of ideas has become as readily accessible as the production of goods. According to Schelsky (1975) we now have a new powerful class of 'meaning producers' performing essential services of information supply. Its power resides in its ability to select and set its own values and goals and apply them in turn to its audience. Because of the prevalence of the mass media, journalists are potentially the most powerful transmitter of values. Research conducted by Cardiff University (Lewis et al., 2008) says journalists 'now produce three times as much copy as they did twenty years ago'.[10] With regard to the role of PR, the researchers find that '60% of press articles (quality broadsheet) and 34% of broadcast stories come wholly or mainly from one of the pre-packages sources' (ibid). An administrative news culture is dominating newsrooms – with journalists sitting behind their desks recycling or regurgitating PR and wire material (also dubbed 'churnalism') – rather than the investigative news culture. Nick Davies' (2008) book and this research do not stand alone: there has been more criticism about the state of journalism and the demise of its professional values (in the case of the United States, see, for example, Kovach and Rosenstiehl, 2001). As we have seen, professional journalism places a premium on news stories based upon what people in power say and do. This removes any doubt about story selection – 'The Prime Minister or President said it so we had to cover it' – and it makes journalism less expensive as reporters have access to the publicity machinery of those in power. Reporters are loathe to antagonize their sources, depending upon them as they do for stories. Indeed, successful politicians learn to exploit journalists' dependence upon official sources to maximum effect. This dependence also makes possible what the modern public-relations industry does in its surreptitious manner.

If journalists raise an issue that no one in power is discussing, they risk being viewed as partisan and unprofessional by attempting to force their own views into the news. Therefore reliance on official sources has a tremendous disciplinary effect on the range of legitimate news stories. It also means the public is at the mercy of those in power to a far greater extent than was the case under partisan journalism.

Adherence to newsroom routines

In one of the earliest studies into newsroom culture, Breed (1955) queried how journalists were made to conform to the editorial policies of their employing organizations. Breed's account showed that their conformity was the result, not of managerial coercion, but of their colleagues' expectations and a strong sense of group attachment. Further evidence of this sort came from research testing White's conclusion that news selection depended on the idiosyncrasies of individual journalists (White, 1950). Comparing intake editors in different newspapers Gieber (1964) found little variation between journalists' judgements about newsworthiness. This implied a marked rigidity in production routines. The conclusion was supported by Sigelman (1973) who found a striking stability in the news worker's environment. Journalists were largely conformist, complying with organizational goals to minimize conflict. Tunstall's (1971) study of specialist correspondents followed Breed by examining reference groups and role expectations but went further to explore journalists' relations with their sources, their colleagues in competing organizations, the goals of their employing organizations, and the wider status hierarchy of specialist journalism. One conclusion was that for it to be manageable, much of news work must be routinized, leading journalists to conform to standardized patterns of reporting and writing. Tuchman (1972, 1973, 1978) came to much the same conclusion about American television and newspaper journalists. Yet her work represents a profound shift in research on news at this point, away from organizational analysis, towards an interest in the social construction of news and the making of meaning. Emerging at the height of anti-war radicalism in the United States and a resurgence of critical media research, Tuchman saw the social organization of news work as enabling the mediation of society's dominant ideas, through the routinized collaboration between news organizations and news. Molotch and Lester's (1974) research reinforced this view, seeing news 'promoters' (sources), news 'assemblers' (news workers) and news 'consumers' (audiences) in a collective process of social construction.

Proprietorial control

In terms of media accountability, the protection of freedom of speech through the first amendment in the United States and common law in the United Kingdom occurred at a time when newspapers and magazines were widely available as the media industry was commercially viable. As publishing became an increasingly lucrative sector during the nineteenth century, market forces enabled the generation of innumerable titles. News entrepreneurs could launch a title with relative ease, ensuring the circulation of a fairly broad range of political viewpoints. Major cities, especially in the United States, might have well over a dozen papers available at any given time.

As the media became such an explicitly commercial enterprise, their driving purpose was to attract increasing numbers of readers – and they did so using techniques that were as inexpensive as possible. Sensationalism, fabrication, bribery and a host of other disreputable activities delivered stories that interested the public but obliterated the legitimacy of journalism in the public interest.

Ironically, as proprietors and emerging media corporations capitalized on big sales, the markets became less competitive as it was harder for smaller enterprises to match the resources or means of the ever-expanding large titles. Media ownership grew ever more monopolistic.

Social and occupational control

While, in liberal democracies, journalists legitimate their professional activity by adherence to the notion of freedom of the Press, there is no agreement or shared definition of what it means. In West Germany, for instance, a distinction is made between external and internal freedom of the Press. External freedom of the Press refers to the independence of the Press from the state; internal freedom of the Press refers to the independence of editors from publishers and owners (Loffler and Ricker, 1986). This distinction does not apply in the United States or United Kingdom. In the United States, the First Amendment's section on free speech defends the media's autonomy as a communicator, while in the United Kingdom it is upheld under European law. But there is nothing in this that protects the journalist from interference by their own editors or their media organization's commercial or political interests. For the most part in the United Kingdom, there is no protection for journalists who refuse to undertake work on the basis of their ethics or conscience.

Views about reporting practices also vary from nation to nation, with no fixed global professional agreement on standards. Renate Kocher (1986) compared approaches in German and British newsrooms and found British journalists in general did not baulk at badgering sources or paying for information, but drew the line at being partisan in their copy. They believed audiences should be presented with the full facts so they can make up their own minds. In contrast, German journalists felt it was justified to oppose extreme political views on the grounds of warning readers and thereby protecting the public sphere. In another study, 45 per cent of German journalists felt it justifiable to give greatest prominence to aspects of a story that supported their personal view (Kepplinger, 1989). For British journalists, professionalism was measured by being first, whereas in Germany it was measured by the depth of coverage.

Ethics must start with individual values

As we have seen, attempts to interfere with journalistic independence, be it from governments, businesses or press officers, are perceived as an attack on professional autonomy. But it may not be as clear-cut and this is why rebuilding trust in the media must start through individual ethics before professional standards can be raised. This is because journalists can in fact exercise some agency. Whether or not this can be divorced from professional identity is a moot point as the agency presented might vary minimally from individual to individual if they are all part of the same social grouping or have been socialized into certain professional norms. In this way, agency might in fact be one way that media institutions help to control their staff and subject them to professional identities. New entrants to journalism need to be aware of this contextual overtone if progress is to be made.

For instance, journalists can exercise agency over their choice of contacts and sources to a degree. This can be tracked and reflected on to examine who they include and omit. Journalists can be inconsistent and can write stories that contradict their earlier assertions or editorial standpoints. In contrast members of the professions have to display consistency, such as in the exercise of legal precedents in court case judgements. News outlets changing their editorial standpoint will claim that they are merely reflecting prevailing views and thereby are acting in the public interest. Unlike professionals, journalists also behave selectively towards the consequences of their actions, in particular the effects of their reporting.

> Journalists will normally accept that positive developments, e.g. the abolition of social grievances, are a consequence of their reporting; but they also normally deny that negative developments, for example the intensification of social grievances, are caused by their reporting.
> (Kepplinger and Kocher, 1990, p. 305)

Examples for this would be the mis-reporting of the risks from MMR vaccines in 2002.[11] The causal links between misreporting and negative consequences on individuals or wider society are much harder to prove than, say, a series of medical blunders by a top physician, which can be re-examined and scrutinized by other professionals.

The point here is that professionalization can come from within when the professionals themselves can exert the control and form the values and norms for the occupation. We have seen how professionalism can also be used by groups outside (owners, state and organizations) as well as within newsrooms to change an occupation and to use it as a system of control and discipline. As Aldridge and Evetts (2003) conclude, the discourse 'professionalism' is used as a tool to separate the producers from the product and change is legitimized by referring to the 'professional' nature of it. Journalists need to reconnect with the practice of journalism and legitimize their own feelings in order to raise standards and preserve professional autonomy.

Can theoretical approaches help rebuild trust?

One way to understand why individual values are fundamental is to look at the founding philosophical underpinnings of ethics. Some of the most abiding textbooks of journalism see ethics as applied rather than theoretical, that is, a set of tools and codes to negotiate. From the time of Aristotle thousands of years ago, philosophers have emphasized ethical decision-making as resting with the individual; ethics must be personal, a matter of free choice rather than conformity to institutional or other group norms (Merrill, 1996).

The professionalization of journalism, with its accompanying codification of ethics and standards, has detached ethical conduct from individual values. Ethics, both in their content and their maintenance, have become institutionalized instead of internalized by editorial staff. Journalism ethics can be thought of as an ongoing negotiation between these two sides of professionalism: between the organizational demands with standards, routines and goals for the media company and the occupational professionalism – values, norms and identity developing among journalists themselves (Örnebring, 2008a). The question is how the current trends in the journalistic profession and in journalistic work influence the balance.

The normative view is that the news media are more transparent than many businesses because their work product is constantly available for scrutiny. Journalists regularly critique and challenge each other's work. In most countries, the consumer has many news choices and can reject those whose standards fall short.

But from a theoretical perspective, ethics can be negotiated and applied in a number of ways that depend upon the culture within which a news organization may operate as well as the overriding motivations and purpose of the outlet. Sociologist Max Weber defines two types of rational behaviour, functional rationality and substantive rationality, which can be usefully applied to journalistic intent. An individual shows 'functional rationality' when 'he orients his actions according to purpose, means and incidental consequences' (Weber, 1973, p. 13). For example, a politician is sometimes faced with conflicting demands and has to choose the best way forward bearing in mind the drawbacks. Weber defines that an individual shows substantive rationality if 'without regards to the foreseeable consequences, his actions are directed by what his convictions of duty, dignity, beauty, religious rites, piety or the importance of "cause" seem to command him to do' (ibid.). In other words, substantive rationality requires behaviour according to the commands or demands the individual feels subject to. He illustrates the concept with journalists who, despite personal ethics, feel duty bound to publish regardless. Side by side with these notions, Weber identifies two types of ethical orientation: ethics of responsibility and ethics of ultimate ends. The former is closely connected to functional responsibility, says Weber, and is shown in those who accept responsibility for the intentional and unintentional foreseeable consequences of their behaviour, which they adapt accordingly. The ethics of ultimate ends, however, is a characteristic of journalists he maintains. Here the individual might be driven by overriding ethical objectives which they feel overrides them taking any responsibility for unintentional but foreseeable consequences.

However, it would be useful to see if there is any link between this individual ethical judgement and decision-making behaviour in newsrooms to try to better our understanding of why things go wrong. One philosophical paradigm of ethical decision making, the consequentialist approach, suggests that the end result of an action or behaviour overrides the concepts of moral right and wrong. There are two basic types of consequentialist theories of ethical decision making: ethical egoism and utilitarianism.

Ethical egoism, as its name implies, views 'right' action as that which emphasizes the individual's personal good. An ethical egoist behaves in an egocentric manner which maximizes individual benefits and while minimizing individual harm (Donaldson and Werhane, 1993). An example might be where a journalist publishes an image of a suicide in a public place to maximize sales.

Utilitarianism is a theory that was popularized by the nineteenth-century philosopher John Stuart Mill. Supporters of this theory argue that moral action is concerned with more than just personal satisfaction. In utilitarianism, 'right' action maximizes the good of the overall human community, as opposed to ethical egoism where individual utility in maximized. A person following a utilitarian approach behaves in a fashion which attempts to maximize the overall desired benefits of society (Donaldson and Werhane, 1993). Therefore, using the previous example, the journalist might decide that publishing the image could act as a deterrent to others. Or they might determine that the impact on the family of the deceased could be more damaging than any possible public interest.

Amidst the pressures of the workplace (Cottle, 1999; Aldridge and Evetts, 2003; Ursell, 2003), journalists continue to challenge the standards for their professional performance. When problems occur the assumption has tended to be that this is a matter of internal managerial concern as happened following the David Kelly affair.[12] The BBC responded by launching a rigorous training schedule in law and ethics for all its editorial staff via its College of Journalism. As in any workplace, journalists work in an environment where certain behaviours are thought to be morally appropriate and others less so. Of this we know little beyond press reports and insider exposés of the more extreme cases. How is ethical journalistic behaviour shaped within a media organization? How are breaches of 'normal' practice handled and contained? Any discussion of individual ethics therefore needs to take into account the culture within which they are enacted.

Culture is a term that was originally developed in the field of anthropology, and has recently become a prevalent research area in organizational studies (Smircich, 1983). Unfortunately, a consistent definition of this ambiguous concept is extremely difficult to find, especially in a managerial context. However, there are certain concepts that are ubiquitous to attempted definitions of culture and one of the more accepted ones comes from Kroeber and Kluckhohn (1952):

> Culture consists of patterns, explicit and implicit, of and for behavior acquired and transmitted by symbols, constituting the distinctive achievement of human groups, including their embodiment of artifacts; the essential core of culture consists of traditional (i.e. historically derived and selected) ideas and attached values.
>
> (1952, p. 181)

For years, scholars have called for research that would explain and analyse the relationship between management, organizations and culture (Evans, 1990). Subsequently, culture is just beginning to be realized as an observable, tangible aspect of human behaviour (Adler, 1986). According to Hofstede (1980, 1984), individualist cultures are societies where people are primarily concerned with their own interests and those of their immediate family. In collectivist cultures, on the other hand, individuals belong to groups or collectivities which look after them in exchange for their loyalty. Lawrence Kohlberg's (1969) work on moral development has made a major contribution to the research on ethical decision-making in organizations focussing on moral judgments and the cognitive processes of individuals confronted by ethical dilemmas. A moral judgment, according to Kohlberg, is essentially the mental determination of right and wrong which is based on values and social judgments involving people. Kohlberg's model of moral development asserts that individuals pass sequentially through one or more different stages as they morally develop. Each stage reflects a level of moral maturity and Kohlberg contends that ethical behaviour can be understood by identifying an individual's relative position on the scale.

Kohlberg's six stages of moral development are subdivided by three exclusive levels. The first level, the 'preconventional level' is where the individual is concerned with his or her immediate interests and does not yet understand the rules and expectations of society. In the second level, the 'conventional level', people recognize societal laws, rules, and expectations. The third level, the 'postconventional' level, is represented by people who accept society's rules only if they agree with the moral foundation that the rules are based upon. Generally, children under the age of nine appear in level I, adolescents and most adults hit their plateau in level II, and only a small percentage of people ever reach the third level of moral development. Research on Kohlberg's model also suggests that moral development is positively related to education and work experience (Colby et al., 1983). In an application of Kohlberg's model to a random sample of graduate business ethics students, Penn and Collier (1985) concluded that 37 per cent of the students moved to a higher moral development stage as a result of ethical training. The major limitation of Kohlberg's model is that it focuses on how individuals reason about ethical matters and not on actual behaviour. In Trevino's (1988) person-situation interactionist model of ethical decision making, individual and situational variables are provided as moderators in the ethical decision making process. Trevino (1988) also purports that factors such as job context, organizational culture, and work characteristics affect decision-making. Moreover, Trevino found that group influences on individual decisions are often an integral part of an organization's culture and can alter the situation in which an individual engages in an ethical decision.

How to re-build ethical accountability?

We need to think of ethics as a negotiation between the individual journalist and the fluid and dynamic contexts within which they work. There are some practical steps that can help build ethical accountability, starting with the individual and radiating out into the organization:

- Building a strong foundation
- Openness rather than objectivity
- Named sources.

The first is through education and training. Journalists need strong ethical foundations if they are to negotiate a host of challenges to their professional autonomy. Firstly they need to reflect why they wish to do journalism. What are their motivations? How do they see journalism's function in society and that of the journalist? What are their values and feelings? By exploring these aspects in depth – whether through immersion in academic or scholarly work in a seminar room or through self-reflection or discussion with others in the field – the entrant will develop lifelong skills of reflexivity. It is reflexivity that makes a student of journalism 'be able' to do the job, rather than just 'know how' (Niblock, 2007). The benefits of pre-entry education in ethics is that it offers a safe space for students to explore the options and take risks while minimizing harm to themselves and others. Whether through role play, though newsroom simulations or through seminar discussion, advance encounters with ethical dilemmas help build a students' sense of self-confidence.

The second is through journalists being open about themselves and their approach to the story. As we saw in Chapter 1, the 'professional' approach to journalism has, since the early stages of the twentieth century, rested on a somewhat slippery notion of objectivity. Journalists are there to be simply trusted and believed because their professional status assumes that they keep themselves out of the story and simply report fairly and without bias, representing the sides of the story with equal balance. But this assumes a scientific approach by which a journalist can apply a wholly non-subjective style, as if a computer or laboratory can determine the 'truth' of a situation. By virtue of their human subjectivity, a journalist will select the angle, sources, descriptions, quotations, supportive evidence for any story. And no two journalists will produce identical copy. A more effective and honest approach is for the journalist to be visible, either by blogging or providing a few details about how they chose to report the story, describing reflexively the process of selection and rejection of evidence and sources. The Internet lends itself particularly well to this technique by allowing the reporter unlimited space in which to insert links in the news article to a parallel narrative. The downside is that in times of diminished reporting time and resources, this might prove time-consuming.

An alternative approach is for journalists to use the techniques of immersionism to position themselves within the story, using the first person 'I' to locate themselves. In this way, it is clear that the story is the product of human decision-making and editorial judgment. This technique is sometimes used in local journalism, where the reporter might indeed be a known figure in the community, as opposed to a distant, anonymous national or international reporter.

At the very minimum, news organizations might publish transparent details about their staff members' political affiliations so that consumers can deduce whether they feel they can trust that source of information. Prominent bloggers often provide substantial information about themselves. It might be dismissed as dull when a journalist or blogger Tweets or writes about mundane every day matters that are not news or are very personal to them. But over time it does build up a picture, albeit partial, of their motivations and interests and humanizes the reporting behind the news.

The rise of the readers' editor or ombudsman has been a significant step towards transparency. For instance the *New York Times'* public editor and The *Guardian's* readers' editor write columns in which they clarify and explain news coverage and invite dialogue and the journalistic conduct of their own organization's reporters. But they are doing the job that the reporters themselves once did when they stepped out of the newsroom and engaged directly with their readerships who would give direct responses, both positive and negative, to their work on the streets of the community they live and work in.

Journalists should also revisit their policies and practices over the third point: naming sources to rebuild confidence in their work. Countless news organizations refer to 'an unnamed source' or a 'source close to' without any discussion as to why they have not been identified. In 1989, *New Yorker* writer Janet Malcolm published her famous essay, 'The Journalist and the Murderer', with its notoriously overheated opening sentence: 'Every journalist who is not too stupid or too full of himself to notice what is going on knows that what he does is morally indefensible.'[13] Some outlets have attempted to establish rules about when it is permissible to use an anonymous source, to hold these occasions to a minimum and to require the reporter to explain why a source was permitted to remain anonymous. Sometimes that is the only way to get important information. But sometimes it is a ruse on the part of the reporter: an anonymous source inside the government sounds more impressive than an assistant. In 1994, Los Angeles County Superior Court Judge Lance Ito threatened to close OJ Simpson's murder trial to television cameras in the wake of one controversial report. KNBC-TV reporter Tracie Savage told viewers that DNA tests showed a match between blood on a sock found in Simpson's bedroom and his former wife's blood. The link was attributed to a source who refused to be named. Defenders of confidential sources say they bring to light important stories that otherwise would never surface. If used carefully, they say, unnamed sources are a valuable tool. But opponents of the practice argue that information from unnamed people further under-mines journalism's credibility yet further. Some editors say many good stories would be missed if there were a prohibition on anonymous sources. Whistleblowers would be reluctant to come forward, as would those whose safety or job may be jeopardized by speaking publicly to a reporter.

> The weakest sources are those whose names we cannot publish. Reuters uses anonymous sources when we believe they are provid-ing accurate, reliable and newsworthy information that we could not obtain any other way. We should not use anonymous sources when sources we can name are readily available for the same information.[14]

Whatever the methods used to increase ethical transparency, they show that far from being a threat to standards, new media technology has mechanisms for enhancing trust. It is not so much the media form as they way the journalist chooses to use it over time.

Conclusion

Journalists' ethical accountability has tended to be based upon the insti-tutional reputation of their parent organization. Individual reporters are seen as representatives of a media company rather than as autonomous practitioners with their own ethical standards and motivations. But this raises some ethical concerns, especially given the scandals unfolding on both sides of the Atlantic, not least the mobile phone-hacking alle-gations in the United Kingdom. A news brand that has, over time, succeeded in gaining public trust does by no means guarantee the standards of practice by its individual journalists.

While the traditional approaches of journalism credibility, ethics and standards are still as important, they are challenged in today's media environment because they have relied for too long on organizational control and external regulation. Journalists' sense of self-identity and thereby their ethical positioning has evolved because journalism is an act rather than a place of work. The role and practices of journal-ism are changing along with the content and so must the way ethical behaviours are owned and enacted. From an occupational standpoint, journalism continually stakes a claim for autonomy, in that its practi-tioners insist they themselves know how to serve the best interests of their public. Self-determination and occupational identity seem to be much more of a driver to individuals to uphold high ethical standards than organizational determination or regulation. Journalists have staked this claim and by reinforcing that zeal and building on that identity, journalists are best placed to act with the highest propriety rather than by seeing themselves purely in light of which organization or outfit they do journalism for.

Perhaps a more useful way to consider media accountability in the age of the Fifth Estate is to refocus on the range and quality of content over the professional status or intention of the producer. To what extent does a story add to the public discourse? Is the information factual, reliable, meaningful or timely at its moment of circulation? In this way, we start to disconnect journalistic accountability from who or what produces the journalism, and instead see journalism as a verb. To 'do journalism' requires individual decision-making and agency on the part of the reporter or producer.

5 Subverting from within: Challenging the Professional Media

Technology is transforming the ways in which audiences receive news and the working lives of those who produce it. The 18–35-year-old generation, who have grown up with the World Wide Web, expect to get their news for free these days. They get it from television, in their email inboxes, on their phones – all at the click of a button. Many believe these changes have huge implications for the future of journalism, especially in terms of public trust and the standards of practice within the trade. As the craft is swept along at high speed on a journey for which it is not fully prepared, the future of journalism is in the here-and-now – multi-platform, multi-skilled and mired in doubt and controversy. As Rushkoff (2003) states: '[t]he best evidence we have that something truly new is going on is our mainstream media's inability to understand it' (pp. 53–4).

But it is wrong to believe that the brave new e-world is bringing down journalism, as many within the industry have argued. Technology can all too easily be made the scapegoat for something more insidious and damaging, which lies at the real heart of doubts about the future of journalism in the digital age.

The skills that media professionals need to survive and succeed have shifted with the evolution of technologies. Today's journalism graduates are walking into a field that is constantly changing because of technology and convergence. The Internet has had a tremendous impact on traditional media outlets. It has been blamed for the downturn in conventional advertising revenue which has led, in turn, as critics say, to closures and redundancies in newsrooms. But the even greater challenge to journalism goes deeper than job insecurity as it questions the very notion of journalism as an exclusive, delineated profession. The Internet has changed the way journalists work. Digital technology has given journalists new tools, and newsroom processes have changed. New forms of outlet – mostly Internet related – have emerged both within the traditional media companies and in new media companies in competition with traditional media. In most media organizations, the Web is still a channel for distribution of content produced for the traditional news media – newspaper, radio and TV. The Web is another way for the audience to listen to radio, to have a look on the newscasts on TV and to read the newspaper. But 'Web journalism' is increasingly becoming its own genre with its own defining characteristics that are shaping the way in which journalism is perceived and practiced. The Web has routines and news selection criteria that differ from traditional outlets, for instance. It is driven by speed and immediacy, so that stories are ongoing and charted as they unfold rather than as a 'finished' piece of text, audio or video. The Web also has a more informal style, supported by interactivity where the audience is engaged through debates.

This chapter will explore how the development of the Web into the primary medium for breaking news has influenced journalists' work and their professional roles. It will examine whether new processes in newsrooms only serve as a more efficient way of producing the same old journalism, or whether professional values also changing.

Online journalism might be viewed by some as a threat to the figure of the media professional. But, importantly, it offers an opportunity to further our understanding of just what a journalist is. In stark contrast to the opinions of those in the industry, technological change as actually been identified for a long time as promoting professionalization. One of the earliest explorations of professionalism stated that technical advance generated growth in the field (Carr-Saunders and Wilson, 1933) and all professions are being drastically affected by the pace and extent of technology, offering specializations or new inventions.

Technology has undoubtedly altered roles, practices and relationships in news production – that indeed is how it has tended to be framed both by industry, accrediting bodies and in turn within how education and training courses are structured and delivered. But this ignores another equally important issue, which is how much the commercial imperative and associated budgetary savings have delimited technology's creative potential into delivering news faster with fewer staff.

Accordingly, this chapter will not be offering an account of the different technological aspects to enhance the skill set of the media professional – there are manuals by experts who can explain that better. Rather it will examine what challenges and opportunities for professionalism emerge.

Issues in online journalism

Let's start by looking at the fears. One school of thought believes the significant decline in newspaper sales since the 1970s means newspapers will soon go out of business; one commentator Philip Meyer predicts ominously that 2043 will be the year when newsprint dies, 'as the last exhausted reader tosses aside the final crumpled edition'. The phone-hacking scandal and the ensuing Leveson Inquiry certainly make many of us fear journalism's standards of accuracy and rigour are also suffering from a terminal illness. The emerging use of 'content' instead of 'news' or 'journalism' to describe material published, posted or broadcast suggests that journalists' work is little more than 'stuff', filling a designated space, rather than the carefully-crafted result of quality reporting. The rise of 'content' over 'news' or 'features' seems to have changed the relationship between editorial staff and the words, pictures, audio and visuals they package. Newsrooms now routinely utilize content management systems. A content management system (CMS) is a computer program that allows publishing, editing and modifying content on a website as well as maintenance from a central page. It provides procedures to manage workflow in a collaborative environment. Serving as a central repository, the CMS raises the version level when new updates are added to an already existing file. Previously flow of content was limited and followed hierarchical structures within the newsroom. Now content is managed within a networked structure, the benefit of which is that it can provide journalists with access to the work produced by colleagues across an entire company. A study of Independent Radio News (Machin and Niblock, 2008) indicated that newsrooms already repackage existing content without adding any new information or reporting. With CMS, the same content is being reused in different titles and repurposed for Web-TV and radio. This, coupled with the fact that journalists are leaving the office less and less, raises questions for professionalism.

CMS also offers pre-programmed templates to which journalists must fit their content. A consistent style of presentation is vital to ensure continuity and familiarity for audience, hence the centrality of 'house style' and design rubrics to newsroom staff. Formats do indeed make it easier for journalists to produce news and for the audience to consume news journalism. There is no doubting that a hallmark of journalism professionalism is meeting a brief and adhering to the tone and protocols of the newsroom. At the same time, digital tools journalists use give them new creative possibilities. This creativity cannot be realized in a fast-paced editorial environment, and standardized formats ease and quicken the production process. Now CMS of newspaper websites have standard layouts so the reporters can write directly into the pages without a sub-editor doing the editing. The formats in newspapers make the pages look the same every day, and in TV and radio news the format leaves very little room for surprise. The most well defined formats are used in online news where the news has to be published immediately. Online news formats are so standardized that the number of characters of the title are prescribed (between 31 and 33 characters). The first four paragraphs of online news have to be suitable for radio and mobile phones (often defining word order and word choice). This was borne out by research into Bloomberg News's template approach to news writing in order to appeal to local and global audiences simultaneously (Machin and Niblock, 2010).

> Particularly when the professional status of an occupation is in dispute, as it is for journalism, its leaders typically claim certain levels of technical performance and standards of community orientation, labeling as 'charlatans' those outsiders who fall short.
>
> (Singer, 2003, p. 140)

As we saw in the previous chapters, there is a general consensus among journalists that Web journalism operates at a standard below traditional news media (Lasica, 2001). On the one hand, the Web allows greater autonomy for journalists, enabling the independent reporter to disseminate his or her work free of any connection to – or constraint from – a media outlet. Ironically, being affiliated to an organization may have been the defining distinction of a professional journalist in the past even though that might also entail a loss of autonomy or full control over the output. Online information distributors claim it is this very autonomy, especially from the business interests of concentrated media power, that is an asset (McClintick, 1998).

Changing market conditions and the intensive competition for dwindling audiences have created new challenges for journalists (MacGregor, 1997; Cottle, 2003; Franklin, 2003). How infrastructural changes impact on news output has been debated in media sociology for some time (e.g. Franklin; 1997; McNair, 1998, 2000). Some feel that the world of news will be turned on its head as 'new technologies re-engineer the relationship between how views and information are exchanged, judged and assigned significance, and how public opinion is formed' (Lloyd and Seaton, 2006, p. 1). As mentioned, the emphasis in public debate has been much more on technology as the cause of change rather than how the industry has chosen to respond to it. There has been little research into the working practices of journalists, tending instead to examine the products of their work, but a growing media sociology interest in journalists' employment conditions suggests that labour-saving production technologies, multi-skilling and the consequently reduced opportunities for team working have a 'de-skilling' effect (Bromley, 1997; see also Cottle, 1999; Ursell, 2003). For better or for worse, new media technologies are said to change the nature of news and the way in which it is produced. The notion of evolving consensus over the qualities and skills belonging to the world of journalism would change as 'technologies of news relay broaden the field of who might be considered a journalist and what might be considered journalism' (Zelizer, 2004a). Evaluating the credibility of a medium as vast, public and popular as the Internet has become increasingly difficult. The Internet has made it possible for people, not only journalists, to search for information and to express themselves in completely new ways. Some academics feel that this blows apart the notion of the media professional:

> The 'knowledge monopoly' of the journalistic profession has been broken, and it is difficult to say who is a journalist and who is not. The borders of journalism are less clear than ever.
>
> (Nygren, 2011, p. 219)

The dip in trust in journalism has been accompanied by the breakdown of another important relationship; one far more threatening to journalistic standards than technology. Media owners and journalists once worked in close union, with a common purpose of producing news that would attract as many readers, listeners and viewers as possible. Journalism, it was felt by both, was the lifeblood of the industry and to dilute the content would not only lose audiences but also the reputation of the industry as a whole. But, a noticeable distance has developed between media proprietors, journalists and audiences, coinciding with the shift from strong publishers and campaigning moguls to executive boards and shareholders. This breakdown of relationships seems to have occurred when small outlets, run by local owners, were sold to corporations. This brought newsrooms better facilities and slick offices and streamlined efficiency. But as years went by, Power once vested in editors and indeed readers became a need to maximize investors' returns. Owners, even when they were chairing a board, were identifiable and personified the ideology of the operation. Today, with one or two notorious exceptions, the ownership of a corporation is anonymous and de-personified. Cost-cutting has reduced the number of correspondents stationed abroad, shrivelled or closed news bureaux and crippled local reporting staff who once kept an eye on governors, mayors, councillors, criminals and the justice system. It has shrunk the size of the typical newspaper page, cutting the cost of newsprint but reducing news content. That so many outlets are fighting for their survival suggests that free-market capitalism is not the ideal platform on which to base the journalism industry. Considering that the sales of the popular press are in greatest decline, despite the slight peak of interest in Murdoch's *Sun on Sunday*, launched to replace the *News of the World*, the message seems to be that news consumers are looking for a brand they can trust. If journalism is to survive, it has to 'assert a specific location within this media sphere, demonstrate that it can deliver a particular form of service to the public, however fragmented and commoditized that public might become' (Conboy, 2004, p. 224).

So journalism faces many challenges – but the hidden truth is that these challenges have less to do with journalism, or even technology, than with the context within which journalism is produced. The economic basis of production has transformed both journalism's processes and its perception by the public and institutions. This, more than anything, needs to be tackled if journalism is to survive and revive. Interactive media technologies actually present a golden opportunity for news-makers and news audiences to reflect on the present state of journalism. In the mid-1980s, when computers revolutionized journalistic practices and transformed the economics of production and distribution, technology posed no threat to news itself. Newspaper circulations had been in decline for the previous 30 years, ever since television had started to play a central role in daily life. But television did not dent the appeal of journalism itself; if anything, it raised the media's global profile. While television supplied visually-impressive footage, certain newspapers understood their role within the burgeoning journalism marketplace: the delivery of broad coverage, deep analysis and opinion. The digital revolution, offers a limitless increase in the amount of information. This is not such much a threat to journalism as a challenge. So let us look at the implications:

The future's 'glocal' – global and local

The Internet gives us access to content from newspapers, television channels, blogs and podcasts from around the world. We are no longer limited to our own national media to frame the news of the world; at the push of a button we can go directly to any corner of the globe and get their local perspective. In a war or uprising we are starting to see something interesting happening. Instead of there being two sides to a story, myriad accounts emerge and the challenge to media used to binaries of good versus bad is how to adequately present that diversity. And as well as its global ramifications, the Internet enables a return to the hyperlocal. It is nothing new but was abandoned in the 1980s in favour of cutting newsroom budgets to boost profits. More investment in innovation, quality and rigorous reporting might lure audiences back to journalism, which in turn may bring back the advertisers who are currently promoting themselves in non-journalistic outlets.

Interactivity

Digital journalism also has the scope to be a two-way conversation between news producer and news receiver. Audiences can enter into dialogue with news providers, rather being passive. Greater interactivity means that online writing tends to be more personal, giving reporters, editors and news anchors the chance to be more human and connect with their audience in deeper ways than the styles that were actually invented to relay dispatches over a very shaky transatlantic cable. This can be very challenging to traditionalists, but journalism is not fixed – it has to be dynamic. History shows that media organizations embrace technology to increase efficiency, reduce costs and maximize audiences but there is evidence that recent developments may – ironically – have the potential to wrest some of that power from the corporations. In the early twenty-first century, networked computers, digital cameras and mobile phones with multiple functions are affordable by ordinary consumers. Digital content, capable of being used across media platforms, can be produced by ordinary citizens as well as professional newsgatherers. This begs the question, 'Would you trust a citizen brain surgeon?' This is a common refrain as the news industry grapples with the idea of a technologically empowered public. Audiences can take a very different and active role within the news-making process, seeking alternative news sources or actively providing content. This reconfigures the relationship between journalism and citizens and raises important questions about its role, status and function in society.

Curation

The *Guardian*, which is owned by a trust rather than a conglomerate, is promoting its open journalism, seeking to work interactively with readers and other partners in what it describes as an open eco-structure of information. Editor Alan Rusbridger sees the role of the paper as to aggregate, curate, and distribute rather than hiding behind pay walls. When covering the Arab Spring, for example, it used a lot more North African writers rather than only its star reporters and translated into Egyptian to widen access. Readers of interactive online news are free, within editorial constraints, to select the stories they wish to read, investigate them in how much depth they want and, potentially, respond to them. Increasingly – and most significantly – news receivers are being invited to share in producing the news content, taking on some of the functions of journalists by circulating information, images, video footage, audio clips and text. Look at recent examples: The 7/7 attacks on London, when the public took over reporting because of news blackouts. The riots, when news crews were forced out over fears they would pass footage to police. Coverage was shaky, exaggerated and fabricated in some instances but an accurate picture soon built up. While broadcasting Goliaths such as Sky News and ITN flew in big-name presenters to riot-stricken cities across England, a couple of Sikh men, armed with a point-and-shoot camera, calling themselves Sangat News, stole the headlines.

Investigations

New technology could revive investigative journalism. Increasing pressure on news outlets to be fast and first means that journalism which is both expensive to produce and time-consuming to gather has a much lower priority than entertainment. The Internet, and the closer rapport it engenders between journalists and their audiences, might serve to regenerate in-depth reporting. There have been experiments such as crowdsourcing. For example, The Sunlight Foundation, a non-profit, non-partisan Washington-based organization, gave tools to citizen journalists so they could find out which members of US Congress employed their spouses. Although it is often viewed as a challenge to the traditional news media, the Internet might better be conceptualized as their complement – supplementing and interconnecting the work of professional journalists with that of citizens. Web-based citizen journalism has the potential to be, as one commentator described it, 'People who are non-journalists committing random acts of journalism', bringing us closer to a vision of the public in the interests of democracy. Not only does this offer a diverse array of viewpoints but it may also take the agenda-setting power out of the hands of a few and into those of the many.

Balance of biases

Interactivity will compromise journalism's impartiality severely, which has been the main argument used against it by mainstream news proprietors. When the public can easily access a wide range of views through the Internet, it is increasingly likely that they will turn away from outlets that fail to reflect their personal opinions. This has led senior broadcasters to propose, controversially, that the BBC embrace the idea of 'radical impartiality', in which public service broadcasters would accommodate the dissemination of a broader range of views. Surely the aim should be to encourage more and more feedback from and engagement with news audiences, who may shape the agenda and potentially provide an important 'check and balance' on the quality and truth of the news? This is less of a problem for newspapers and independent websites, which are allowed to adopt editorial standpoints, and which might open the way for newspapers to capitalize. Objectivity can be complemented by transparency. Before stepping down as prime minister, Tony Blair made a speech criticizing the British media, during which he singled out the *Independent* newspaper as a 'metaphor' for what happened to the news during his tenure, saying it was 'well-edited and lively' but 'avowedly a viewspaper not merely a newspaper'. The 'red issue' of May 2006, guest-edited by Bono from U2, was perhaps the most famous of the Independent's front pages, and drew attention to what some see as the skewed news values of many media outlets. It combined the headline 'No news today' in yellow text on a red background with a much smaller subheading at the bottom of the page, which read, 'Just 6,500 Africans died today as a result of preventable, treatable disease'. News outlets must ask themselves what they can provide that people are willing to pay for. Selecting and explaining key news items would appear to be a sensible shift for the industry – look at what the *Guardian* achieved over *WikiLeaks* and phone hacking. Though it has to be said – those peaks in sales were short lived.

Educating the online mindset

Digital media and, more recently, multimedia newsrooms are also transforming the training and education of journalism worldwide (Castaneda, 2003). It has inspired training programmes and universities across the globe to develop modules and courses devoted to the practice and theory of journalism in a 'new media' environment. The sheer range of approaches and models of teaching and researching multimedia reveal one thing at least: multimedia means different things to different people (Boczkowski, 2004). Wise (2000) claims digital media, new media, information and communications technologies, Internet, interactivity, virtuality and cyberspace are all used interchangeably with multimedia. The combination of mastering newsgathering and story-telling techniques in all media formats (so-called 'multi-skilling'), as well as the integration of digital network technologies coupled with a rethinking of the news producer-consumer relationship tends to be seen as one of the biggest challenges facing journalism studies and education in the twenty-first century (Bardoel and Deuze, 2001; Pavlik et al., 2001; Teoh Kheng Yau and Al-Hawamdeh, 2001). But perhaps the starting point for module or programme design is to take a step back from skills and to encourage students to reflect on what convergence really means to those oft-cited yet elusive basic tenets of journalistic autonomy.

The platform convergence process poses two particular challenges to mainstream news organizations; one idea is that it threatens a news culture that prefers individual endeavour over teamwork and knowledge-sharing (Singer, 2004). You only have to think of journalism movies' traditional view of the heroic, autonomous reporter working doggedly day and night to deliver a scoop to their editor's desk. Colleagues are also competitors, each fighting for the coveted front-page splash. The idea of a networked journalism where 'ownership' or production of a story might be shared amongst several journalists or non-journalist contributors is a seismic shift away from how most journalists have been trained.

The second major qualitative change is about editing and selection. Professional accounts and the literature suggest that new media technologies challenge one of the most fundamental 'truths' in journalism, namely: the professional journalist is the one who determines what publics see, hear and read about the world (Fulton, 1996; Singer, 1998). Whereas a journalist in the past might have been trained to write a single story, now the emphasis has shifted from single-authored copy to multi-authored packages. The organizational features of converged newsrooms impact on the competences of journalists operating in these environments. Huang et al. (2003) are among many who saw the shift away from single authorship to team-based journalism, with reports of resistance from established news staffs.[1] Research among reporters in various converging newsrooms in the United States by Singer (2004) and Boczkowski (2004) shows similar experiences, citing conflicts and resistance to the notion of sharing information. A survey by multimedia consulting firm Innovation – commissioned by the World Association of Newspapers and conducted in 2001 among media executives worldwide – cited as the biggest obstacle to media convergence 'the individualistic nature of journalists' (mentioned by 31 per cent of all respondents). As well as creating tensions between colleagues, the introduction of new technology in newsrooms has thrown up evidence about the ways news personnel and management are responding. It certainly appears, from studies in the United Kingdom and elsewhere in Europe, that some media outlets are being uncreative in their use of technology, preferring to standardize and routinize news production (Niblock, 2010; Nygren, 2011).

Journalism practiced outside the mainstream offers some of the most interesting avenues for student journalists fascinated by interactivity rather than the top-down model. It is known by a range of titles including citizen journalism, participatory journalism, open-source journalism, personal media and grassroots reporting. The newer generations of citizen journalism are built on the groundwork by pioneering developers such as Slashdot, Indymedia, and, later, the South Korean OhmyNews, which in 2003 was 'the most influential online news site in that country, attracting an estimated 2 million readers a day' (Gillmor, 2003, p. 7), These sites emerged in tandem with the ubiquity of social networking sites and Web 2.0. They then drove technical developments even further in response. But while technology offered new platforms, a key cultural factor was behind the emergence of citizen journalism – the perceived shortcomings of mainstream media. 'As the mainstream media space, particularly in the United States, becomes increasingly centralized and profit-driven, its ability to offer a multiplicity of perspectives on affairs of global importance is diminished' (Rushkoff, 2003, p. 17). Citizen journalism's intention, claim its advocates, is to fill the spaces abandoned by the mainstream.

Citizen journalism's practices differ markedly from those of the mainstream news industry, however. For the most part, its proponents have realized that, as Bardoel and Deuze put it, 'with the explosive increase of information on a worldwide scale, the necessity of offering information about information has become a crucial addition to journalism's skills and tasks. . . . This redefines the journalist's role as an annotational or orientational one, a shift from the watchdog to the "guidedog" ' (2001, p. 94). Further, citizen journalism places ordinary citizens rather than salaried journalists in that orienteering role, writing and submitting stories which are less frequently the outcome of direct investigative reporting, and more often collects and collate available information on certain newsworthy topics. The practice here is similar most of all to that of industry journalists compiling stories from a variety of news agency feeds and combining it with further evaluation and commentary.

'Agenda watching' not 'gatekeeping'

The raw materials of a great deal of day-to-day collation journalism, bar exclusive interviews or material, are accessible by all regardless of whether you are a professional journalist or not. One underlying principle of citizen journalism is one of agenda-watching: citizen journalists engage in the continued observation of the output gates of key institutions and organizations as well as of news outlets, and the gathering and compilation of those items of information which are relevant to the story at hand (for a detailed description of this process, see Bruns, 2005). In their reports, citizen journalists – as gatewatchers and information 'guidedogs' – focus more on publicizing the availability of important information than on publishing new stories, in other words, and rely on their readers to draw their own conclusions from such reports as well as the source information they link to.

Rebuilding trust?

One of the big contentions from mainstream practice is that editorial oversight of this process remains limited or indeed absent. On the one hand, the agenda-watching process could be seen as requiring less policing as it builds on information available elsewhere; 'bad' stories are thus easily identified by editors and readers as they often quite obviously misrepresent the sources they use. This is quite different from traditional journalism, where the accuracy or appropriateness of a journalist's use of, say, a press release from a company in developing their story is difficult to confirm for readers unless they have direct access to the source information. One reason why the citizen journalism process is viewed as more trustworthy by its advocates is that users, rather than paid editors, evaluate submitted stories and respond via fora/message boards. This, some argue, is a more reliable and transparent system, involving greater numbers of people for verification rather than a single editor. The actual process varies on different citizen journalism sites. While some sites (such as *Slashdot* or *OhmyNews*) retain the role of traditional content editors, if in a strictly limited fashion, some (such as *Kuro5hin* or *Plastic*) allow all registered users to comment and/or vote on submitted stories before they are 'officially' published, while others (such as most Indymedia sites) publish all submitted stories automatically, leaving it to their users to debate and evaluate the quality and veracity of news stories through commentary and discussion functions attached to each story. Further, especially in wiki-based sites such as *Wikipedia* and *Wikinews* it also becomes possible for users to continue to edit and improve stories after publication.

Post-publication filtering and editing is by necessity a collaborative effort, and today takes place predominantly through comments and discussion – users may provide further information and references which extend, support, or contradict details of the original story. They may comment on the summary of information provided in the article, or they may provide alternative points of view to those espoused in the story itself. It clearly involves having faith in the power of citizens to arbitrate as opposed to the traditional 'top down' system of editing that simply asks the reader to trust the professional editor. Frequently, such discussion and debate is significantly more detailed than the story which sparked it, showing that in citizen journalism the primary focus is on such discursive engagement more than on the mere provision of facts; as Chan describes it in her study of *Slashdot*, 'highlighting the expertise of users and the value of their participation, news reading shifts from an act centred on the reports and analyses of news professionals and designated experts, to one often equally focussed on the assessment and opinions of fellow users on the network' (2002).

News production in such environments, in other words, is community based; it 'proceeds from a logic of engagement founded upon notions of production and involvement rather than consumption and spectacle' (Gibson and Kelly, 2000, p. 11) and therefore deserves the description as participatory, citizen journalism. Users in such environments are always also invited to be producers of content; indeed, the boundaries between the two roles are increasingly blurred and irrelevant. As we will see soon, it becomes more useful to describe their role as that of a hybrid user-producer, or produser (Bruns, 2008). This supports Gillmor's observation that 'if contemporary American journalism is a lecture, what it is evolving into is something that incorporates a conversation and seminar' (2003, p. 79). At its best, such discursive citizen journalism – found in dedicated citizen journalism Websites as much as in the even further decentralized, distributed discussions of the news blogosphere – approaches what Heikkilä and Kunelius postulate as deliberative journalism:

> [D]eliberative journalism would underscore the variety of ways to frame an issue. It would assume that opinions – not to mention

majorities and minorities – do not precede public deliberation, that thoughts and opinions do not precede their articulation in public, but that they start to emerge when the frames are publicly shared.

(2002)

Further, it realizes a challenge for journalism which was first set by Gans in 1980: 'Ideally, . . . the news should be omniperspectival; it should present and represent all perspectives in and on [a story]' (1980, p. 312). This relies on the view that anyone can and should be trusted to be both creative and responsible.

Hence we can think of the news story now as a process rather than a product, which is a huge leap away from the commercial model that sees news as a commodity (Machin and Niblock, 2008.) No longer can news be neatly divided into finalized versions, editions, and issues as it was in the traditional news arena. *Kuro5hin*'s Rusty Foster likens it to a factory production line: 'the way journalism right now works in the mainstream media is an industrial process: . . . You collect raw material from sources, and then you package it into a product and you deliver it to eyeballs. It's a very neat, very simple, very nineteenth century way of thinking about doing things' (Foster, 2001).

The online model of media professionalism

The online journalism model media professionalism can be characterized thus:

- Community evaluation not top down
- Not about finished stories/products, but about ongoing process
- Shared common property rather than a commodity.

Online journalism has a distinctly different ethos and methodology from industrial production – which has important implications for news and journalism. By seeing journalism as a process rather than as a story, it ends the traditional product cycle. Its outputs are no longer discrete versions of products with individual stories representing all that is known about a given event at the time of publication. Instead, citizen journalism offers a series of ongoing and potentially never-ending revisions, more in common with a wiki entry than a traditional model of news presentation. Interactivity fundamentally alters the relationship between the journalist and user, as Shirky says,

In changing the relations between media and individuals, the Internet does not herald the rise of a powerful consumer. The Internet heralds the disappearance of the consumer altogether, because the Internet destroys the noisy advertiser/silent consumer relationship that the mass media relies [sic] upon. The rise of the Internet undermines the existence of the consumer because it undermines the role of mass media. In the age of the Internet, no one is a passive consumer anymore because everyone is a media outlet.

(2000)

Ethics and law online

Thomas Jefferson said some 200 years ago that if he had to choose between government without newspapers or newspapers without government, he 'should not hesitate a moment to prefer the latter'. It was this vision of how a democracy should work that prompted the framers of the US Constitution to make free expression the first amendment of the charter's 'Bill of Rights'. In reality, the amendment simply said that Congress cannot enact a law infringing free speech or a free press. That brief clause has been the beacon and the shield for the American press for over two centuries, but it is not carved in stone for eternity. It is tested almost daily in the courts, on the streets, and in the corridors of power. But the professional mantra of neutrality and even the pursuit of a scientific objectivity may be hard to achieve in citizen, collaborative journalism.

One key foundation the Internet threatens is public interest. Surveys of audiences and journalists seem to suggest is that it is too simple to think that there is one public 'out there' who can be satisfied with one fits-all definition of public interest. In diverse communities, different publics, or audiences with differing contexts co-exist – be they faith-related, age-defined, socio-economic or educational. There is always the possibility of something being 'in the public interest' for one section of the population, yet jarring with another. Therefore it is hard to reach a consensual notion of the public interest, particularly when social attitudes shift so rapidly. In the 1950s, it was possible to sue the media for defamation if they accused you of being gay. Nowadays, only very few in Western society would view homosexuality as a slur.

This has led senior broadcasters to make a controversial proposal that even the BBC embrace the idea of 'radical impartiality'. Public service broadcasters would accommodate the dissemination of a broader range of views than they had previously. Shortly after the murder of the Pakistani opposition party leader Benazir Bhutto on December 2007, the BBC's journalists uploaded a story of the events on the corporation's award-winning news website. As commentators and spokespeople speculated that certain Islamic opponents of Mrs Bhutto might have been behind the killing, website users began to post their feedback to unfolding events using the *Have Your Say* forum. Days later the BBC's Head of News, Peter Horrocks, revealed that his interactive team had considered switching off a facility on the forum that allowed users to recommend their favourite feedback comments. Many of the top 20 recommended posts were damning of Islam, causing great concern and forcing journalists and moderators to make difficult editorial judgements. As Horrocks later reflected:

> It was only a fleeting suggestion but that we could consider, however briefly, freezing this important part of the BBC News' service tells you something about the power and the potential danger of the new intensity of the interaction between the contributing public, journalists and audiences.
>
> (2008)

This example is one of many happening every day in the journalistic media that highlight the issues arising from the rapid development and wide scale deployment of interactive forms of news making in Britain.

In his blog, Horrocks argued for the dissemination of 'views that are rigorously tested, but with respect for all legally expressed opinions'. In actual fact, this deviates little from the editorial impartiality guideline which necessitates a wide array of represented voices, myriad opinions colliding, confirming and contrasting with one another.

Though any discussion of professional journalism ethics has to be prefixed by the fact that organized, paid-for journalism has also severely compromised its own standards and is in no way insulated from ethical breaches by virtue of its professionalized status.

At the time of writing, an independent newsgathering organization, the Bureau for Investigative Journalism based at City University, London, has come under heavy criticism for its reporting of child sexual abuse at North Wales care homes which was featured on a BBC2 Newsnight edition. The BBC Director General George Entwistle has just resigned. The key issues for ethics in this type of collaborative journalism include who is to enforce standards, and who is liable when breaches occur. In online journalism, the question of legal liability remains unclear in a large co-produced project with anonymous contributors.

Conclusion

In the digital age, there are many uncertainties about what lies ahead for journalism. Despite the huge transformations we have already witnessed, we are still probably far closer to the beginning of the online revolution than we are to the end. In fact it is questionable whether any end can be in sight as technology propels us into previously inconceivable domains. The debate over the future of journalism in the multi-platform converged media world is fraught with uncertainty. Any discussion can only be based upon opinion rather than on fact, and views are divergent. One school of thought believes newspapers will soon be out of business, a 'traditional' medium relegated to the past. With it, they fear, will go the standards of accuracy and rigour upon which journalism is based. With significant declines in newspaper sales in particular over the past 30 years – and some predict this is terminal. Others say the death of journalism is far from inevitable – for it is the 'content' that counts.

But the e-generation and new technology aren't the danger. Digital developments have arisen amid media consolidation and mergers and at a time when corporations allow a news-as-commodity approach to dominate production values and editorial strategies. The Internet and its associated journalisms are trying, albeit haphazardly, to fill a gaping news chasm which opened long before the first website was launched, the first podcast uploaded and the first blog posted. They are an important reminder that journalism has always been an annoyance, a scurrilous activity, operating on the borders of society, in dark recesses where ordinary people fear to delve. Its practitioners have never done the job to be liked or admired. The routine practices of news editors and reporters were not invented in one fell swoop. They arose and evolved from particular circumstances and philosophies. And they are still arising and evolving, thanks to the opportunities that technologies bring. Journalists themselves are understandably wary about the new online environment, but more due to the ever greater demands placed on them by managers rather than the technology itself. In the future, as has been proven in the past, they will find a way to accommodate these changes for the benefit of the public interest.

6 Towards the New Media Professional

In a 2008 survey, one anonymous UK editor described what they were now looking for from new recruits:

> People who have the traditional skill-set (shorthand, law, court reporting etc.) but are also capable of writing for web with SEO in mind, experience of UGC and comment moderation, video shooting and editing and other specialist software knowledge. On top of this, we need all our people to use the internet and other forms of digitised media as part of their daily lives – and recognise the value of social networking sites etc. to traditional media. If our staff don't 'live' the internet they won't really understand it – which will make adapting to the new platforms almost impossible. So we need people with advanced but day-to-day internet knowledge.
>
> (Skillset, 2008)

This dizzying array of requirements crystalizes just what a confusing, challenging situation awaits any would-be journalist trying to complete an application form or construct their CV. Anyone hoping to enter the editor's newsroom would need to have a vast arsenal of skills at their disposal – and at an advanced level – to work across innumerable media platforms at speed and with ease. If an entry-level candidate needs to present this amount of expertise for their first job in journalism, their three-year undergraduate course plus postgraduate training would have to be pretty intense to ensure they can turn out competent videos, superfast shorthand speeds, be able to challenge a judge in a court of law as well as work with citizen journalists and maximize search engine optimization.

But if you look again, it might equally be argued that this statement gives nothing away about what the ideal candidate let alone the industry really *needs*. There is a vast difference between *knowing how* to do something – knowing which button to press – and *being able* to make significant editorial decisions about what should be covered and how.

When confronted with menus of requirements from the industry like this – and you can find equally detailed demands and condemnation of existing graduate standards in journalism industry forums – it is inevitable that many in education will take note and strive to instil this proscribed media professionalism into their courses. They will write programmes that seek to reflect the pressures of working life in different parts of the media industry, with a focus on high-pressure experience, working to deadlines, managing complex projects and taking clear responsibility for the work that is produced and communicated. According to the industry, degree courses should do as much as possible to replicate a professional media environment, with lots of contact between students and people who have worked in the media industries, offer the best preparation. Forget critical analysis, they say; what these students need to know about is the day-to-day pressures of turning around packages, websites, recordings, interviews, features, reports, and the whole plethora of items that a media business produces hour-by-hour.

The idea that graduates will be ready for work and will be able to step into the world of daily deadlines, hierarchies and workplace political positioning, almost without any transition or reorientation, is prevalent. But is that really be best way to cultivate the attributes and qualities needed to *be able* to make a sustained and polished contribution to the current and future sustainability of journalism? As we saw in Chapters 1 and 2, professionalism in a course is often measured by accreditation and almost certainly by its close association with the media industry. Programmes gain a premium if they are backed by a professional body, taught by a leading industry practitioner-turned-professor, and the cultural mindset students are encouraged to foster is all too often about mirroring a fairly restricted view.

This issue here is that learners, even in a university's humanities, media or liberal arts environment, are being asked to assimilate a view of professionalism that is external to their experience, and are assessed on those external values and principles. The transformation of the journalism industry really needs the hearts and minds of talented individuals who embrace and embody a strong set of personally held values.

Changing media, changing mindsets

It does not take this book to tell you that the techniques and tools of what it means to be a media professional are changing. While the Web is buzzing the flurry of apps, devices and job titles, what is boils down to for journalism is two significant and far-reaching cognitive shifts:

Firstly, as Chapter 1 showed, advances and ease of access to technology have broken up the traditional means of production and in turn the definition of the media professional. It happened long before the Internet was cited as a 'threat' to traditional media as far back as the late 1970s when desktop-based media production applications and workstations blurred and merged role boundaries. This meant that industry professionalism was no longer defined solely on the basis of access to exclusive resources like studios and print presses. With diverse and accessible media hardware and software offering merely tools of news reporting and dissemination, surely the focus should be on reinvigorating journalism as a mindset and a set of cognitive processes, not just as a set of skills. While the array of tools available has expanded, their ease of use should not be used as a way of obscuring or concealing the real crisis: that of journalists' role in society.

Secondly, and building on this point, the wide availability of more social ways to communicate demands a far more open and transparently reflexive relationship between journalists and their publics – and with one another. Journalists are now in a position to account for and explain their editorial decision-making, and have it questioned or even challenged directly by peers, sources and the public. The traditional 'top down' approach of newsmakers deciding what their audiences should be interested in and how they should be told has been replaced by interactivity, with journalists needing to take strong decisions while still having the flexibility and accountability to adapt to given change.

Both developments open up and demystify the process of media production, showing that 'insider-status' is not the defining characteristic but that being a media professional is focused on generating content in a creative, engaging manner, and building relationships of trust with audiences. What it should not be about is regressive work-based hierarchies, closed shops and restrictive working practices. The Leveson Inquiry in the United Kingdom has ensured that the once-concealed process of producing journalism is now more open to scrutiny and observation from audiences than ever before.

The questions for journalists, students, employers and educators are what values, qualities and attributes are essential to work successfully in the new media world? Then, once identified, how can these values be cultivated and inculcated in the next generation of journalists? Whether they are innate, taught or developed through experience, how do we measure these attributes?

Speaking to employers, the upsurge in new media forms and challenges to the traditional model of journalism means they are now looking for something more in addition to the traditional capabilities required of entrants such as writing skills or shorthand speeds. Particular attitudes, approaches and knowledge are in greater demand – even more so than certain skills – as employers seek to build sustainability. One perspective is that universities and other training providers must adapt their provision from one that foregrounds skills to foregrounding critical thinking in order to build these attributes. Another view is that educators should only recruit students who already display a predisposition to media work, believing strongly that only a few people possess the essential qualities.

Where professionalism and training intersect

If professionalism must move away from pre-conceived notions of the 'ideal' employee into a more fluid, diverse and attribute-based approach to recruitment, then universities will need to significantly change their approach. The shift to university-based delivery may have closed off other recruitment grounds and disadvantaged potentially excellent recruits from accessing media careers. Moreover, universities and colleges should encourage a more diverse of intake and build greater confidence on the part of students, not just prime them with skills.

As we have seen, the last quarter-century has heralded a significant increase in the size and nature of graduate entry into the media. The so-called 'massification' of higher education has continued even into postgraduate training for journalists, with the net effect that employers of all kinds – global and local – are looking for recruits who are prepared to work readily and confidently across several roles and media at any time of the day or night. Increasingly, that mindset must embrace working with geographical flexibility as town or city-centre newsrooms are replaced by remote working. The professionalized nature of the industry means news outlets want employees who can assimilate organizational values, and are prepared to operate amidst the uncertain technological and cultural demands of the twenty-first century newsroom. The hope is that these new flexible, multi-skilled employees will become the leaders of the future, sustaining the journalism industry for generations to come.

Some recruiters use the term 'media mindset' to describe an individual whose outlook naturally fits with the heavy demands of a rapidly changing workplace. Attributes such as curiosity, passion, persistence and dogged determination are often cited as essential characteristics for anyone hoping to launch a successful media career. A couple of recent studies have attempted to draw out what that mindset might consist of.

A UK-wide survey in 2008, revealed that almost three – quarters of employers (71 per cent) said there was a skills gap among graduates entering journalism. The report by Skillset, the Sector Skills Council for the Creative Media Industries (now Creative Skillset) found that employers across all sectors expect graduates to be able to work across multiple platforms. The first of its kind in UK publishing, the convergence survey was conducted in partnership with the National Council for the Training of Journalists (NCTJ), Broadcast Journalism Training Council (BJTC), Periodicals Training Council (PTC) and Society of Editors.

Of particular concern to respondents were perceived lacks in traditional skills such as finding stories, use of language, writing, media law, shorthand and newsgathering. In particular, the standard of written English among new entrants was flagged both in the survey and interviews with editors as a major cause for concern.

The most pronounced gap for all employers surveyed, no matter the medium, was initiative. Too few new entrants to journalism have the capacity to generate their own story ideas and follow them through, they said. This, followed closely by use of language and written skills, was seen as the biggest hurdle to overcome in recruiting and inducting new journalists. The survey then went on to prioritize the other skills editors found lacking in new recruits. Significantly these were the traditional skills and knowledge associated with journalism since long before digital technology had an impact on day-to-day working. Knowledge of media law, shorthand, newsgathering and time management were ranked much higher priority than audio or video skills, for instance.

While the study focuses and lists the skills editors want to see in new recruits, closer analysis of the survey results, especially the qualitative interviews with journalists, reveals a number of qualities, values and attributes that editors are really searching for: notably, communication skills, curiosity, attention to detail and a willingness to challenge authority. This may be a more useful way to examine the data in order to draw out the attributes of professionalism in order to prepare for a media career.

Communication

One manager interviewed said:

> In these days of hyper-locality, even on BBC websites, it is essential that novice journalists know how to cultivate grass-roots contacts, as well as ferret out news angles. They need to be taught how to lose their deference to the press releases which are part of their daily diet and to bring more of a critical analysis to the lines with which they are increasingly being spoon-fed by the PR machines.
>
> (Skillset, 2008)

Evidence of a lack of direct communication is journalists placing too much reliance on online sourcing instead of making calls.

Questioning

Connected to this, editors are concerned that journalists are shy of questioning or challenging sources. One editor said:

> We have noticed the alarming growth of a spoon-feeding culture in recent years where trainees are entirely happy to wait for emails from PR departments which are then unquestioningly regurgitated in papers and websites. Healthy scepticism underpinned by solid basic journalistic skills should be the aim.
>
> (Skillset, 2008)

They are not probing or sufficiently challenging. One said: 'They will get a sound bite but there is often a much better story or sound bite if people dig deeper.' Another editor said secondary questioning was a 'dying art'. He said: 'They find out what the basic story is about and tell it through quotes from one or two people. Stories are "thinner". They lack detail.'

Curiosity

One respondent to the NCTJ survey remarked that new recruits are less driven than they once were and are less likely to take the initiative and generate exclusives, preferring to take a more passive approach in the newsrooms and waiting for handouts or instructions.

Flexibility

There was broad consensus across the views of interviewees that the skill sets of print journalists and broadcast journalists are becoming more similar. The view was also articulated that all sectors are looking for new entrants who are comfortable working across two or three different platforms in the course of a working day. They now expect staff to be able to move seamlessly around the production of text, photographs, video and audio. This suggests the new media professional needs to have a flexible attitude to media formats and does not prioritize a specific preference. This is important given that some higher education programmes are still medium specific. Most employers do not state an expectation for the new entrant to come fully skilled, but they certainly demand the mindset and basic knowledge to be in place. Their message to providers is encapsulated in the comment that '[i]f colleges and universities want to run good courses, they have to recognise that they will need to build web skills into every aspect of teaching journalism.'

One prominent theme across the survey, which was identified by the authors, was that editors want candidates to embrace the 'traditional values' and 'basics of journalism'. However, these values and basics are not defined by interviewees.

> The ability to hold on to the traditional values of journalism while modernising around the new platforms
>
> We would expect people to have a very good knowledge about the basics of journalism.
>
> (Skillset, 2008)

They are able to be quite specific about the new technical abilities they wish entrants to possess in various degrees, but not the underlying qualities. If editors could express these more accessibly to young people, it might help to demystify the traits they are seeking. Moreover, these comments by editors do not in any way acknowledge the impact that major newsroom budget cuts have had on practice. Rather they signal that it is merely technology that has wrought change instead of how the underlying commercial imperative has dramatically affected journalists' capacity to even leave the newsroom.

It is also time to unpack the actual meanings of terms that are used unquestioned in journalism such as 'good stories', repeated often in answers to the survey.

> The ability to find stories and tell people about what you have found is still the most important part of journalism. No amount of converging will compensate for a lack of good stories.
>
> (Skillset, 2008)

What constitutes 'good stories' will inevitably be medium- and outlet-specific depending on the target audience and the particular tone or priority of the outlet. Perhaps it is time for journalists who defend 'traditional values' to openly and transparently deconstruct some of the so-called instinctual 'nose for news' statements that form the basis of recruitment and explain what they really constitute on the ground. There are numerous accounts of what makes news, though few account for the fact that it is commercial pressures and production values that can determine whether a story is selected or not for publication, broadcast or upload (Niblock, 2005). This can be learnt. Editors should be up front and transparent about this. Moreover, journalism courses need to educate students to be able to analyse media to unravel their target market and how to address them most effectively whether story or source selection or forms of presentation and interactivity.

One respondent at least acknowledges the challenge in preparing new recruits for the mastery of skills and knowledge required:

> It is a difficult task, but teaching the traditional skills must be maintained while cultivating multi-media talent as well – and both to a high standard. The traditional should not be downgraded to accommodate the 'sexy'. The basics are needed for whatever medium is being used.
>
> (Skillset, 2008)

However, one significant contradiction was in editors stating that the delivery of public affairs – the operation of local, central and international governance – is no longer as much of a priority to them as it once was. In response, one accrediting body the National Council for the Training of Journalists, cut its syllabus down in 2011. It is difficult to reconcile this with maintaining 'basic values' of journalism.

Looking ahead, the survey's key points were that journalists are going to have to work harder across more media with fewer safeguards between them and their audience. They cite the skills of accuracy and capable writing as essential, not least because the journalist will be writing straight to publication as the number of production journalists, especially sub-editors who proofread, has been significantly cut to make savings. So while accuracy and clarity reflect journalistic ethical principles, in the context of the evermore financially constrained journalism environment they are being cited not as moral standards but as cost-saving conveniences.

Another broader survey of employers was undertaken by the Council for Industry and Higher Education (Diamond et. al, 2011). The study places particular emphasis on global employability, but has been widely embraced by news providers such as the BBC who offered CIHE a platform at the BBC College of Training conference for educators in 2011. In a similar way, they identified 'soft' skills such as team working, communication and respecting others' values, but unlike the previous survey saw these qualities as more crucial than any technological skill.

CIHE's researchers asked employers from a range of industries to rank 'global competencies' in order of importance. At the very top of the list – with almost unanimous agreement of its urgency – is 'an ability to work collaboratively with teams of people from a range of backgrounds and countries' followed closely by 'excellent communication skills; both speaking and listening' (ibid.). More than anything else, it seems employers are looking for strong team players and communicators.

If we look at the first attribute, working collaboratively with a variety of people requires the ability to understand and embrace a variety of values and perspectives. As one journalist put it when applying the findings to the media later:

> You need to be able to put yourself in the mind of the person you are speaking to and think about what is important to them. The same goes for your readers and listeners; their values and interests might be quite different from your own but you have to reflect them by asking the questions they would ask and sourcing the voices they would appreciate.
>
> (interview with author, June 2012)

The mental agility to see differing perspectives is essential if media outlets are to thrive in the competitive conditions of the digital age. New professionals need the flexibility to adapt to rapidly changing contexts, to garner new audiences while serving the interests of their existing markets.

Collaboration and teamwork

The CIHE study emphasized the ability to work in partnership with people from a variety of cultures and backgrounds. Similarly, media working requires bringing together diverse teams of people. Collaboration is imperative for media leaders so that they can interact effectively with others and drive the operation forward. Journalists must be able to relate to people at all levels, from different backgrounds, because sources and audiences come from all walks of life including people of the opposite gender, different ethic, social and religious backgrounds.

Adaptability, drive and resilience

Behaviours most synonymous with adaptability are commonly emphasised by employers. Journalists and other media workers often find themselves working in unfamiliar situations, whether physical, such as using new piece of technology or going to a new location, or sociocultural. Experts say that a strong sense of self-awareness helps people to adapt, because they have a clear understanding of how they relate to and are perceived by others.

Adaptability also extends to being able to work in different locations, relishing the opportunity for variety or exploration. By being willing to be relocated where they are most needed, workers are able to respond better to market demands. People who are mobile, whether geographically or culturally, do require resilience so that they can adapt with minimal stress to uncertainty or setbacks when things do not go to plan.

Drive is characterized by people who are self-starters and do not wait to be told what to do. Being independent minded, creative and a thinker are valued assets who will make a real difference by virtue of their initiative. Self-motivation is a combination of will power, goals and ability to continue attaining the highest level of success. In his 1954 book, *Motivation and Personality*, Abraham Maslow made an attempt to provide an answer to why some people are highly driven through his breakthrough theory of motivation. Maslow studied the traits and practices of exemplary people, such as Albert Einstein and Eleanor Roosevelt, for his data. He suggested a series of stages of motivation. The lowest level (Level 1) comprises the basic survival needs of the body such as food, shelter and clothing. The moment the basic needs are met, the needs of the mind arise; these are more complex and therefore, elusive. 'I am all right now but will I have enough for tomorrow?' is the first mind-created need, which Maslow terms as Level 2, the need for safety. Responding to this need to a reasonable length is wise, but it can take over our life until we find ourselves saving for five generations down the line. Fulfilling this need could become a bottomless pit, if not checked. Level 3 relates to social needs such as the need for love, for family, for belonging. Social needs can only be met through our interaction with others, and they are therefore avenues for generating stress, for we have little control over how others view us. Level 4 refers to the need for self-esteem, achievement, mastery, independence, status, and respect. While some of the components such as self-esteem or achievement is inner driven, the value that society places on us, or what we do, can make us externally dependent. The company's whizz kid or the public's favourite hero is uneasily aware of the precariousness of their position. One hears of top executives having heart attacks when the next general board meeting is scheduled, top stars having nervous breakdowns when a new star emerges on the horizon and they find their 'position' threatened. At the highest level (Level 5), which is that of self-actualization, one works because one's spirit wishes to express itself. When we work at this level, driven from within, we fulfil our life's purpose. Painters are known to have painted on continuously without eating or sleeping, fired with passion. Musicians sing and compose for hours together, lost in their pursuit, unmindful of hunger, thirst or sleep.

In comparison, the Skillset survey suggests that newsrooms are still looking primarily for skills rather than qualities. Or editors at least articulate qualities in terms of the skills by which they are manifested or measured. One of the problems with journalists' articulation of the perceived gap between graduates and the needs of the workplace is the apparent lack of explanation of the principal attributes that lie behind mastery of these skills. This may be one of the reasons why it is claimed many students leave colleges and universities with skills yet do not find employment directly within the media. Certain foundations need to be laid so that the skills of recognizing stories and writing well for audiences are realized. This is the key difference between 'knowing how' to do something and 'being able' to do it. While the Skillset survey explains what would-be journalists need to be able to 'do', the CIHE survey explains the levels of self-awareness and development needed to 'be able' to perform those tasks capably – and to understand why they need doing a certain way.

Can these skills and attributes be learnt or taught?

To operate professionally in the digital sphere, graduates need to develop a blend of attributes as well as skills and knowledge:

- Self-reflexivity
- Critical thinking
- Self-awareness
- Confidence
- Communication
- Initiative
- Values

But the question is how.

Certainly, universities are now being judged more and more on employment outcomes for their students, and it seems employers feel that universities and colleges need to work harder to develop these behaviours before their graduates enter the jobs market.

What can students do?

Students have the greatest interest in, and power over, preparing themselves for the global economy and twenty-first century workplaces. They are undoubtedly responsible for making the most of opportunities presented by schools and universities as well as seeking out their own valuable learning endeavours.

Experiential learning

Students should immerse themselves as much as possible in experiential learning, whether through student journalism or work placements. Interacting with diverse teams of people is viewed as am important way to cultivate a more flexible and resilient outlook.

Community engagement

Activities such as volunteering, fundraising or networking in the local community are highly desirable additions to a media worker's CV. One senior broadcast producer said:

> Although I make programmes for a global audience, I would be very excited to interview a recruit who said they'd been doing work in their local community. In fact I would be distrustful of anyone who wasn't engaged with the place where they live. It shows character, curiosity and the ability to engage with people from all walks of life.
>
> (interview with author 2011)

What can employers do?

Engage future talent

Employers need to engage with future talent as early as possible and build aspirations in order to attract and inspire future staff. One way to do this is by providing role models and mentors from the existing workforce who can share reasons for their own success.

Build well-structured work placements

Designing a well-structured work placement with clear objectives can help to inspire and to instil the values of the media industry. With scores of young journalists clamouring for a limited number of jobs each year, landing that media internship has become a critical career step. While some internships come with a stipend, many are being offered with no pay. Increasingly, both interns and media professionals are asking whether young people are being exploited by these unpaid internships and whether they are keeping those from lower income families out of jobs? Unpaid internships are a widely acknowledged part of the media industry and are considered to provide the experience and 'foot-in-the-door' necessary to get on the career ladder. However some companies have used this to their advantage, taking on interns in unpaid positions, which are usually three to six months long but can be ongoing. A recent survey from the National Union of Journalists (NUJ) found that, of those who did post-qualification work experience, one out of five undertook a placement for three months or more, with some working for over six months unpaid. Further results showed that more than 80 per cent of those on a placement had their work published or broadcast during their work experience. However, 82 per cent of these students did not receive any payment for their work.[1]

Clearly, unless you have enough income at your disposal to work for free, usually in an expensive city, placements only advantage those with the means at their disposal and even more so the employers. But there other ways to grab the attention of potential employers and demonstrate your professional qualities.

Instead of placements, another option is to take a more entrepreneurial approach and demonstrate real-world skills through developing a strong presence of the Web. You might aim to set up and run a site that could be your ideal employer's direct competition, to provide tangible evidence of drive and market-savviness.

Employers working with higher education

It is time to end the mutual distrust between large sections of the journalism industry and the academy. This has become especially acute in the United Kingdom during the Leveson Inquiry, although earlier chapters show that disdain towards higher education has existed for decades. A rift emerged between the academics who are members of the campaign group Hacked Off – signatories to various letters and submissions to the Inquiry – and journalism educators who are actively involved in the day-to-day delivery of professional programmes.

A group of 20 academics called on Lord Justice Leveson to bring in an independent press regulatory body underpinned by statute. Journalism commentators reacted with vitriol against university courses and rounded upon journalism educators in general. This vitriol was encapsulated at the ensuring Society of Editors annual conference in Belfast. There are 'too many courses', there is 'too much media studies' and, 'people who can't do journalism teach it.'

The Leveson Inquiry was a missed opportunity to build media–education relations. Look around at any other professionalized occupational area and what you see is a strong relationship between higher education, research leaders and those industry partners. But the reaction on various message boards and water cooler discussions about the 'most senior 20 media academics' was a sense that they as well as those prominent erring journalists had also got it wrong about ethics.

At the time of writing, a new regulatory body is being discussed and formed. One important, urgent improvement should be to build a bridge between the news industry, training, education and research for the betterment of standards, to rebuild public trust and to keep journalism independent of political influence. Imagine a situation where erring editors are fined so heavily and punitively but where those fines go into training and education, to enabling diverse intake of new journalists, of being proactive to prevent bad reporting in the first place?

No one in either the academy or the industry is suggesting this yet it is the most glaringly open loop in the so-called professionalization of journalism. The gloss of professionalization has permitted the news industry to operate at the heart of the establishment unfettered. But this is no profession, it is a practice, albeit undertaken in most cases under institutional auspices. As with any practice, our focus on ethics should be on the consequences. As long as the consequences are tough then a reconstituted and much more robust and proactive self-regulatory body can implement it.

Imagine how trust could be rebuilt if that body not only acted to resolve and adjudicate over disputes but was an international leader in research into ethical practices and a promoter and educator?

What can higher education do to develop media professionalism?

There is no doubt that the quality and relevance of pre-entry university training and education has come under immense scrutiny. As they are paying so much, students expect more from their programmes, not least a job at the end of it, and employers are keen to ensure that the calibre of graduates emerging matches their requirements.

While some media employers define the role of universities and colleges narrowly as training candidates for news and media jobs, educators should make it their goal to improve the practice of journalism and thereby the democratic society in which it is rooted. Other professions have established required graduate degrees that allow the academy to play a more meaningful role in preparing new employees and thereby helping to develop the defining ethos in their respective areas. If the training task is merely technical and skills based then universities and especially students are subsidizing a role that industry would otherwise have to assume to create a productive entry-level workforce.

The role of the university is somewhat larger and should be focused on the interests of wider society, not merely the market leadership interests of employers. As such, courses should promote and deliver the means for journalists to report effectively and critically in the democratic community. As we saw in the previous chapters, the early advocates of journalism education had high ideals for university education to raise standards and ethics, not merely to reproduce existing norms and conventions. These conflicting goals, embodied by the diversity of individuals tasked with the undertaking, has created tensions both within academic departments and between those staff and their employers over the definition and practice of journalism education.

While the media profession should become much more actively involved with universities, helping to shape curricula and mentor staff and students, at the same time university and college lecturers need to develop a shared disciplinary perspective. The overt split – widening since the Leveson Inquiry – has, to a great extent, impacted on the ontological and epistemological development of journalism studies. There is distrust and disaffection among academics towards one another based on to what extent their background or approach is industry-facing, the notion being that an industry-facing educator must necessarily be at odds with the critique of journalism and vice versa. There should be clearer leadership of the journalism discipline to help practitioner- and theory-led academics forge productive alliances, and to encourage closer working relations with the media for mutual benefit.

Education and training in journalism certainly faces untold challenges if it is adequately prepare students who can lead the next stage of development of the industry. This is especially so as financial support for higher education teaching and research declines. It is important that universities still remain independent from the editorial organizations they work with. As institutions are obliged to look to private and corporate sources for support, they are vulnerable to having their mission co-opted and distorted.

Embedding employability in learning

While almost all universities and colleges offer support to students with careers advice services providing assistance with CV writing and job covering letters, developing employability skills and capabilities is primarily achieved through the degree programme itself. Module content needs to focus on these 'core competences' in areas such as negotiating and influencing, communication, team working and presentation skills. Some academics have found this shift towards industry-facing delivery somewhat problematic as it would seem to downplay the validity and relevance of academic skills to employability.

However, senior figures in global brands such as the BBC have gone to pains to promote essay writing and academic research as essential transferrable skills for successful media working. One editor said:

> You can be taught a range of media skills in the work place pretty quickly. But writing academic papers and essays develops incredibly relevant skills in researching, communication and most of all in arguing and defending a position. Given that in TV, some programmes can sit on the shelf for years before a network is willing to take a risk and broadcast them, it takes incredible skills of diplomacy and persuasion to sell an idea. I think essay writing, which must embrace and evaluate different viewpoints and argue a position, is an excellent grounding.
>
> (interview with author 2011)

Debating

One of the key ways to build confidence in students is through debating, believed to be one of the reasons why private school students appear to progress their careers faster in the top universities and media. Giving students opportunities for verbal discussion, to present ideas to their peers and to give and receive criticism constructively is confidence raising. It also mirrors one of the main ways power is exercised in newsrooms.

Self-reflection

For the media to survive the storms of recent years, wrought not just by technology but a crisis over its standards and public trust, then there need to be a revising of media professionalism. The characteristics of media professionalism are too important for the public interest to be defined by a corporatized media industry. Rather, they need to be determined and promoted through networks with the public interest at their heart. Higher education can play a significant role by offering students a space to reflect not only on the values of their intended profession but how they position themselves in relation to it. This can be achieved not just through deep immersion in journalistic practice but through study, debate and reflection. Likewise, if the industry is committed to raising standards and realigning itself with the public who mistrust it so much, it too should work alongside higher education and to engage and embrace future journalists from a young age.

Ultimately, media professionalism cannot be sustained as a set of externally driven behaviours. History has shown how the media have sought to align themselves with other professions both to raise standards but especially to insulate and protect journalism from accusations of profiteering. The gloss of professionalism has been superficial. It has in some ways been useful for media workers seeking recognition but ultimately they have been denied real authorship of their work and have been delimited by the structures of their parent organizations seeking to maintain the status quo.

Furthermore, the model of professionalism has not protected the public from serious ethical breaches. Newsrooms have hugely undermined their own industry and damaged the lives of many beyond measure. Moreover, they have used the argument of professional independence to deflect calls for greater regulation.

The rise of the Fifth Estate has shown that journalism is no longer an elite quasi professional exclusive domain. Instead, the best way to conceive of journalism is as a set of practices or as a verb. The doing of journalism has become more important than who does it, the product more important than where it appears or who 'owns' it. By this model, so the origins and notions of media professionalism must shift to one that is embodied and embraced by the producer of media messages.

Media professionals need to wholly embrace a set of values and ideals. It is no good journalism training providers delivering the tenets of professional codes if the recipients of that instruction are not offered the chance to negotiate and debate the precepts. Crucially, they need to configure their own values and think why it is that they want to be a journalist. If serving the public interest is not at the heart of what they do – whether they are delivering sports bulletins or hard news – then something is missing.

Journalism departments need to raise their profile and lead discussions on the purpose of journalism, engaging not only students and fellow scholars but also the public. Employers need to work with universities and students together to consider the qualities of the journalism professional.

Notes

Preface

1. However, it is pretty clear that in the United Kingdom, power actually became so concentrated in the tabloid press that it effectively has gone unchecked. The police didn't hold the tabloids to account, and politicians actually courted Rupert Murdoch.

1 From 'Trade' to 'Profession'

1. See http://www.rics.org/site/download_feed.aspx?fileID=2911&fileExtension =PDF.
2. See http://opendepot.org/134/1/thurman_forums.pdf.
3. See http://www.pressgazette.co.uk/tim-luckhurst-statutory-regulation-british-newspapers-would-create-constitutional-absurdity.
4. See http://www.guardian.co.uk/media/2012/oct/17/ken-clarke-leveson-press-regulation.
5. See http://www.independent.co.uk/news/media/press/redtop-redemption-why-tabloid-journalism-matters-2318346.html.
6. See http://www.tasa.org.au/uploads/2011/05/Nolan-David-Session-19-PDF.pdf (p. 10).

2 Preparing Media Professionals

1. See http://www.nctj.com/about-us/our-history.
2. See http://www.ajeuk.org/2011/04/04/survey-of-hackademics-published/.
3. Free school meals eligibility criteria.

3 The Journalistic Self

1. See http://www.spectator.co.uk/features/8744591/what-the-papers-wont-say-2/.
2. See http://www.dailymail.co.uk/news/article-2223348/Britains-vibrant-Press-curbed-says-Boris-Top-Tories-warn-PM-state-regulation.html.

4 Media Accountability

1. O'Grady v. Superior Court of Santa Clara County (2006). See https://www.eff. org/files/filenode/Apple_v_Does/H028579.pdf (p. 1457) (accessed August 19, 2013).
2. See http://www.mediawise.org.uk/www.mediawise.org.uk/files/uploaded/ PCC%20History%20and%20Procedural%20Reform.pdf.
3. See http://www.newscientist.com/article/dn17889-copycat-suicides-fuelled-by-media-reports.html.
4. See http://www.prospectmagazine.co.uk/magazine/peter-kellner-yougov-trust-journalists/.
5. See http://www.bbc.co.uk/journalism/ethics-and-values/accountability/.
6. See https://www.facebook.com/pages/National-Association-of-Citizen-Journalists/187942526527?sk=info.
7. See http://www.societyofeditors.co.uk/page-view.php?pagename=Conference News&parent_page_id=139&news_id=3434&numbertoprintfrom=11& language={language}.
8. See http://www.ft.com/cms/s/0/df217f82-50f1-11e1-8cdb-00144feabdc0. html#axzz2A2OuR0OD.
9. See http://www.inthesetimes.com/article/2427/.
10. See http://www.cardiff.ac.uk/jomec/resources/QualityIndependenceofBritish Journalism.pd.
11. See http://www.ncbi.nlm.nih.gov/pubmed/16808699.
12. See http://www.newyorker.com/archive/2003/12/08/031208fa_fact2.
13. See http://www.newyorker.com/archive/1989/03/13/1989_03_13_038_TNY_ CARDS_000351367.
14. See http://handbook.reuters.com/index.php/The_Essentials_of_Reuters_ sourcing.

5 Subverting from within: Challenging the Professional Media

1. Tampa Bay Online (TBO.com) in the United States where the convergence process met with the resistance of reporters, who did not want to give up their established way of doing things, and in particular refused to work in synergy with colleagues in other parts of the media organization (Stevens, 2002).

6 Towards the New Media Professional

1. See http://www.nuj.org.uk/innerPagenuj.html?docid=1754.

References

Adler, N. J. (1986) *International Dimensions of Organizational Behavior*. Boston, MA: Kent Publishing Co.

Aldridge, M. and Evetts, J. (2003) 'Rethinking the Concept of Professionalism: The Case of Journalism', *The British Journal of Sociology* 54(4): 547–564.

Allison, M. (1986) 'A Literature Review of Approaches to the Professionalism of Journalists', *Journal of Mass Media Ethics* 1(2): 5–19.

Altheide, D. (1976) *Creating Reality: How Television News Distorts Events*. Beverley Hills, CA: Sage.

Bantz, C. R. (1985) 'News Organizations: Conflict as a Crafted Cultural Norm', *Communication* 8: 225–244. in Tumber, H. (1999) News: A Reader, Oxford: Oxford University Press, pp. 134–142.

Barber, B. (1965) 'Some Problems in the Sociology of the Professions', in Kenneth S. Lynn and editors of Daedalus (eds) *The Professions in America*. Boston, MA: Houghton Mifflin.

Bardoel, J. and Deuze, M. (2001) ' "Network Journalism": Converging Competencies of Old and New Media Professionals', *Australian Journalism Review* 23(2): 91–103.

Barthes, R. (2009) *Mythologies*. London: Vintage Classics.

Bell, D. (1973) *The Coming of Post-Industrial Society: A Venture in Social Forecasting*. New York: Basic Books.

Boczkowski, P. (2004) 'The Processes of Adopting Multimedia and Interactivity in Three Online Newsrooms', *Journal of Communication* 54: 197–213.

Borden, S. L. and Bowers, P. (2008) 'Ethical Tensions in News Making: What Journalism has in Common with Other Professions', in Wilkins, L. and Christians, C. G. (eds) *The Handbook of Mass Media Ethics*. London: Routledge.

Breed, W. (1955) 'Social Control in the Newsroom: A Functional Analysis', in Social Forces 33: 326–335 in Tumber, H. (1999) News: A Reader, Oxford: Oxford University Press, pp. 79–84.

Bromley, M. (1997) 'The End of Journalism? Changes in Workplace Practices in the Press and Broadcasting in the 1990s', in Bromley, M. and O'Malley, T. (eds) *A Journalism Reader*. London: Routledge.

Bruns, A. (2005) *Gatewatching: Collaborative Online News Production*. New York: Peter Lang.

Bruns, A. (2008) *Blogs, Wikipedia, Second Life, and Beyond: From Production to Produsage*. New York: Peter Lang.

Carey, J. (1980) 'The University Tradition in Journalism Education', *Carleton University Review* 2(6): 3–7.

Carey, J. (2000) 'Some Personal Notes on US Journalism Education', *Journalism* 1(1): 12–23.

Carr-Saunders, A. M. and Wilson, P. A. (1933) *The Professions*. Oxford: Clarendon Press.

Castaneda, L. (2003) 'Teaching Convergence', Online Journalism Review 6 March 2003, http://www.ojr.org/ojr/education/1046983385.php.

Chalaby, J. (1998) 'The Media and the Formation of the Public Sphere in the New Independent States', *Innovation: The European Journal of Social Sciences* 11(1): 73–85.

Chan, A. (2002) *Collaborative News Networks: Distributed Editing, Collective Action, and the Construction of Online News on Slashdot.org*. Unpublished M.Sc. Thesis. Cambridge, MA: MIT.

Christiansen, C. H., Backman, C., Little, B. R. and Nguyen, A. (1999) 'Occupations and Well Being: A Study of Personal Projects', *American Journal of Occupational Therapy* 53: 91–100.

Cohen, S. and Young, J. (eds) (1981) *The Manufacture of News*. Beverley Hills, CA: Sage.

Cokley, J. and Ranke, A. (2011) 'There's a "Long Tail" in Journalism Education Too', in Franklin, R. and Mensing, D. (eds) *Journalism Education, Training and Employment*. London: Routledge, pp. 159–176.

Colby, A., Kohlberg, L., Gibbs, J. and Lieberman, M. (1983) 'A Longitudinal Study of Moral Judgment', *Monographs of the Society for Research in Child Development* 48(1/2): 1–124.

Coldron, J. and Smith, R. (1999) 'Active Location in Teachers' Construction of their Professional Identities', *Journal of Curriculum Studies* 31(6): 711–726.

Conboy, M. (2004) *Journalism: A Critical History*. London: Sage.

Cooper, S. D. (2006) *Watching the Watchdog: Bloggers as the Fifth Estate*. Washington: Marquette.

Cottle, S. (1993) ' "Race" and Regional Television News: Multi-culturalism and the Production of Popular TV', *New Community* 19(4): 581–592.

Cottle, S. (1999) 'Watching the Watchdogs: Sociologists on Journalism', in Jones, M. and Jones, E. (eds) *Mass Media*. Basingstoke: Macmillan, pp. 97–100.

Cottle, S. (ed.) (2003) *Media Organization and Production*. London: Sage.

Davies, N. (2008) *Flat Earth News*. London: Chatto.

Dear, J. (2010) 'Government cuts make journalism more elitist', http://jeremydear.blogspot.co.uk/2010/08/government-cuts-make-journalism-more.html (accessed August 19, 2013).

Department of Communities and Local Government (2008, updated 2012) 'Tracking economic and child income deprivation at neighbourhood level in England: 1999 to 2009'. https://www.gov.uk/government/publications/tracking-economic-and-child-income-deprivation-at-neighbourhood-level-in-england-1999-to-2009 (accessed August 19, 2013).

Deuze, M. (2005) 'What Is Journalism? Professional Identity and Ideology of Journalists. Reconsidered', *Journalism* 6(4): 442–464.

Diamond, A., Walkley, L., Forbes, P., Hughes, T. and Sheen, J. (2011). Global graduates into global leaders. http://www.cihe.co.uk/global-graduates-into-global-leaders/ (accessed September 22, 2013).

Dickinson, R. (2007) 'Accomplishing Journalism. Towards a Revived Sociology of a Media Occupation', *Cultural Sociology* 1(2): 189–208.

Donaldson, T. and Werhane, P. (1993) *Ethical Issues in Business*. NJ: Prentice Hall.

Donsbach, W. (2004) 'Psychology of News Decisions: Factors Behind Journalists' Professional Behavior', *Journalism* 5: 131–157.

Durkheim, E. (1957) *Professional Ethics and Civic Morals*, translated by C. Brookfield. New York: Routledge.

Eliasoph, N. (1988) 'Routines and the Making of Oppositional News', *Critical Studies in Mass Communication* 5(4): 313–334.

Elliott, P. (1978) 'Professional Ideology and Organisational Change: The Journalist since 1800', in Boyce, G., Curran, J. and Wingate, P. (eds) *Newspaper History from the 17th Century to the Present Day*. London: Constable.

Epstein, R. M. and Hundert, E. M. (2002) 'Defining and Assessing Professional Competence', *JAMA* 287(2) 9 January: 226–235.

Ericson, R. V., Baranek, P. M. and Chan, J. B. L. (1989) *Negotiation Control: A Study of News Sources*. Milton Keynes: Open University Press.

Erikson, E. H. (1968) *Identity: Youth and Crisis*. New York: Norton.

Evans, W. M. (1990) *Organizational Theory*. New York: Wiley.

Fishman, M. (1980) *Manufacturing the News*, Austin: University of Texas Press.

Foster, R. (2001) 'The Utter Failure of Weblogs as Journalism', *Kuro5hin*, http://www.kuro5hin.org/story/2001/10/11/232538/32 (accessed August 13, 2013).

Foucault, M. (1979) *Discipline and Punish: The Birth of the Prison*. London: Vintage.

Franklin, B. (1997) *Newszak and News Media*. London: Arnold.

Franklin, B. (2003) 'A Good Day to Bury Bad News? Journalists, Sources and the Packaging of Politics', in Cottle S. (ed.) *News, Public Relations and Power*. London: Sage.

Franklin, B. and Mensing, D. (eds) (2011) *Journalism Education, Training and Employment*. London: Taylor & Francis.

Friedson, E.. (2001) *Professionalism: The Third Logic*. Cambridge: Polity Press.

Frith, S. and Meech, P. (2007) 'Becoming a Journalist: Journalism Education and Journalism Culture', *Journalism* 8(2): 137–164.

Fulton, K. (1996) 'A Tour of Our Uncertain Future', *Columbia Journalism Review* (March/April), http://www.cjr.org/year/96/2/tour.asp.

Gans, H. (1979, 1980) *Deciding What's News: A Study of CBS Evening News, NBC Nightly News, Newsweek, and Time*. New York: Vintage Books.

Gaukroger, S. (2012) *Objectivity: A Very Short Introduction*. Oxford: Oxford University Press.

Gee, J. P. (2001) 'Identity as an Analytic Lens for Research in Education', *Review of Research in Education* 25: 99–125.

Gee, J. P. and Crawford, V. (1998) 'Two Kinds of Teenagers: Language, Identity, and Social Class', in Alvermann, D., Hinchman, K., Moore, D., Phelps, S. and Waff, D. (eds) *Reconceptualizing the Literacies in Adolescents' Lives*. Mahwah, NJ: Erlbaum, pp. 225–245.

Gibson, J. and Kelly A. (2000) 'Become the Media', *Arena Magazine* 49: 10–11.

Gieber, W. (1964) 'News Is What Newspaperman Makes It', in Dexter, L. A. and White, D. M. (eds) *People, Society, and Mass Communication*. Newark, NJ: Free Press.

Gillmor, D. (2003) 'Foreword', in Bowman, S. and Willis, C. (eds) *We Media: How Audiences Are Shaping the Future of News and Information*. Reston, Va.: The Media Center at the American Press Institute, http://www.hypergene.net/wemedia/download/we_media.pdf.

Glasgow Media Group. (1976) *Bad News*. London: Routledge and Kegan Paul.

Glasgow Media Group. (1980) *More Bad News*. London: Routledge and Kegan Paul.

Glasser, T. L. (1992) 'Professionalism and the derision of diversity: The case of the education of journalists', *Journal of Communication* 42(2): 131–140.

Golding, P. and Elliott, P. (1979) *Making the News*. London: Longman.

Goldthorpe, J. H. with Llewellyn, C. and Payne, C.(1980) *Social Mobility and Class Structure in Modern Britain*. Oxford: Clarendon Press.

Greenslade, R., (2009) 'How journalism became a middle class profession for university graduates', http://www.theguardian.com/media/greenslade/2009/jul/21/newspapers (accessed September 22, 2013).

Hallin, D. C. (1997) 'The Media and War', in Corner, J., Schlesinger, P. and Silverstone, R. (eds) *International Media Research – A Critical Survey*. London, New York: Routledge.

Hanna, M. and Dodd, M. (2012) *McNae's Essential Law for Journalists*. London: Oxford University Press.

Hanna, M. and Sanders, K. (2010) 'Should Editors Prefer Postgraduates? A Comparison of United Kingdom Undergraduate and Postgraduate Journalism Students', in Franklin, B. and Mensing, D. (eds) *Journalism Education, Training and Employment*. London: Routledge.

Hanna, M. and Sanders, K. (2012) 'Perceptions of the News Media's Societal Roles How the Views of UK Journalism Students Changed during Their Education'. *Journalism & Mass Communication Educator*, 67(2), 145–163.

Harcup, T. (2011) 'Research and reflection: supporting journalism educators in becoming scholars'. *Journalism Practice*, 5(2), 161–176.

Heath, A. and Payne, C. (2000) 'Social Mobility', in Halsey, A. H. with Webb, J. (eds) *Twentieth Century British Social Trends*. Basingstoke: Macmillan.

Heikkilä, H. and Kunelius, R. (2002) 17 July, 'Access, Dialogue, Deliberation: Experimenting with Three Concepts of Journalism Criticism', *The International Media and Democracy Project*, http://www.imdp.org/artman/publish/article_27.shtml.

Henningham, J. P. (1979) 'Kyodo Gate-Keepers: A Study of Japanese News Flow', *International Communication Gazette* 25(February): 23–30.

Hofstede, G. (1980) *Culture's Consequences: International Differences in Work-Related Values*. Beverly Hills, CA: Sage.

Hofstede, G. (1984) *Cultural Consequences: International Differences in Work Values*. Beverly Hills, CA: Sage.

Horrocks, P. (2008) The Value of Citizen Journalism, http://www.bbc.co.uk/blogs/theeditors/2008/01/value_of_citizen_journalism.html (accessed September 22, 2013).

Huang, E., Shreve, S., Davis, T., Nair, A., Bettendorf, E., Davison, K. and Meacham, A. (2003) 'Bridging Newsrooms and Classrooms: preparing the next generation of journalists for converged media', paper presented to the 86th Annual Convention of the AEJMC, Kansas City, 30 July–2 August.

Jacobs, R. J. (1996) 'Civil Society and Crisis: Culture, Discourse, and the Rodney King Beating', *American Journal of Sociology* 101(5) March: 1238–1272.

Johnson, T. (1972) *Professions and Power*. London: Macmillan.

Kaplan, R. (2002) *Politics and the American Press: The Rise of Objectivity, 1865–1920*. New York: Cambridge University Press.

Keeble, R. (1998) *The Newspapers Handbook* (second edition). London: Routledge.

Kemmis, S. (1998) in 'Hämäläinen, K. & Siirala, E. (1998). 'Interrupt and say: Is it worth doing. An interview with Stephen Kemmis'. *Lifelong Learning in Europe*, 3(3): 154–60.

Kepplinger, H. M. (1989) 'The Changing Functions of the Mass Media: A Historical Perspective', *Gazette* 44: 177–189.

Kepplinger, H. M. and Kocher, R. (1990) 'Professionalization in the Media World?' *European Journal of Communication* 5: 285–311.

Kerby, A. P. (1991) *Narrative and the Self*. Bloomington: Indiana UP.

Kielhofner, G. (2007) *Model of Human Occupation: Theory and Application*. Baltimore: Lippincott Williams & Wilkins.

Kocher, R. (1986) 'Bloodhounds or Missionaries: Role Definitions of German and British Journalists', *European Journal of Communication* 1: 43–64.

Kohlberg, L. (1969) 'Stage and Sequence: The Cognitive- Developmental Approach to Socialization', in Goslin, D. (ed.) *Handbook of Socialization Theory and Research*. Chicago: Rand McNally.

Kovach, B. and Rosenstiel, T. (2001) *Elements of Journalism: What Newspeople Should Know the Public Should Expect*. New York: Random House.

Kroeber, A. L. and Kluckhohn, C. (1952) *Culture: A Critical Review of the Concepts and Definitions*. Cambridge: Harvard University Press.

Larson, M. S. (1977) *The Rise of Professionalism: A Sociological Analysis*. Berkley, CA: University of California Press.

Lasica, J. D. (2001) 'A Scorecard for Net News Ethics', *Online Journalism Review*, 20 September, http://www.ojr.org/ojr/ethics/1017782140.php.

Leigh, D. (2007) Anthony Sampson Chair Inaugural Lecture, 1 November 2007, http://www.docstoc.com/docs/74943932/in-this-lecture—Lecture-given-by-David-Leigh_-Anthony-Sampson_sdt=0%2C5 (accessed August 19, 2013).

Lewis, J., Williams, A and Franklin, B. (2008) 'Compromised Fourth Estate? UK News Journalism, Public Relations and News Sources', *Journalism Studies* February 2008.

Lippman, W. (1920) *Liberty and the News*. New York: Harcourt, Brace and Howe.

Lloyd, J. and Seaton, J. (2006) *What Can be Done? Making the Media and Politics Better*. Oxford: Blackwell.

Loffler, M. and Ricker, R. (1986) *Handbook of Press Law*. Munich: Beck.

MacGregor, B. (1997) *Live, Direct and Biased? Making Television News in the Satellite Age*. London: Arnold.

McClintick, D. (November 1998) 'Town Crier for the New Age', *Brill's Content* 1(4): 112–127.

McCormick, C. and Pressley, M. (1997) *Educational Psychology: Learning, Instruction, Assessment*. New York: Longman.

McManus, J. H. (1994) *Market Driven Journalism: Let the Citizen Beware*. Thousand Oaks, Calif.: Sage.

McNair, B. (1998) *The Sociology of Journalism*. London: Arnold.

McNair, B. (2000) *Journalism and Democracy: An Evaluation of the Political Public Sphere*. London: Routledge.

McNair, B. (2005) 'What Is Journalism?', in de Burgh, H. (ed.) *Making Journalists: Diverse Models, Global Issues*. London and New York: Routledge, pp. 25–43.

McQuail, D. (1992) *Media Performance: Mass Communication and the Public Interest*. London: Sage.

McQuail, D. (2003) *Media Accountability and Freedom of Publication*. Oxford: Oxford University Press.

Niblock, S., & Machin, D. (2007) 'News values for consumer groups The case of Independent Radio News, London, UK'. *Journalism*, 8(2), 184–204.

Machin, D. and Niblock, S. (2010) 'The New Breed of Business Journalism For Niche Global News: The Case of Bloomberg News', *Journalism Studies* 11(6): 783.

Marjoribanks, T. (2000) *News Corporation, Technology and the Workplace: Global Strategies, Local Change*. Cambridge: Cambridge University Press.

Marr, A. (2004) *My Trade*. London: Macmillan.

Mead, G. H. (1934) *Mind, Self, and Society*. Chicago: University of Chicago Press.

Mensing, D. (2011) 'Realigning Journalism Education', in Franklin, B. and Mensing, D. (eds) *Journalism Education, Training and Employment*. London: Routledge.

Merrill, J. C. (1996) *Existential Journalism*. Ames: Iowa State University Press.

Merritt, D. (1995) 'Public Journalism: Defining a Democratic Art', *Media Studies Journal* 9(3): 125–132.

Millerson, G. (1964) *The Qualifying Associations: A Study in Professionalization*. London: Routledge & Kegan Paul.

Millward, N., Mark, S., David, S. and Hawes, W. R. (1992) *Workplace Industrial Relations in Transition*. Aldershot: Dartmouth Publishing.

Mindich, D. (1998) *Just the Facts: How 'Objectivity' Came to Define American Journalism*. New York: New York University Press.

Mishler, E. G. (1999) *Storylines: Crafts Artists' Narratives of Identity*. Cambridge: Harvard University Press.

Molotch, H. and Lester, M. (1974) 'News as Purposive Behavior: On the Strategic Use of Routine Events', *Accidents, and Scandals in American Sociological Review* 39(1) February: 101–112.

Morrison, D. E. and Tumber, H. (1988) *Journalists at War: The Dynamics of News Reporting during the Falklands Conflict*. London: Sage.

National Union of Journalists (NUJ). (2007) Shaping the Future: Commission On Multi-Media Working. December 2007.

Niblock, S. (2005) 'Staying Calm Under Pressure: The Role of the News Editor', in Keeble, R. (ed.) *Print Journalism: A Critical Introduction*. London: Routledge, pp. 95–104.

Niblock, S. (2007) 'From "Knowing How" to "Being Able": Negotiating the Meanings of Reflective Practice and Reflexive Research in Journalism Studies', *Journalism Practice* 1(1): 20–32.

Niblock, S. (2010) NCTJ News Writing Survey. Presentation of results to NCTJ Journalism Skills Conference December 2010.

Nichols, J. T., & McChesney, R. W. (2005) *Tragedy and farce: How the American media sell wars, spin elections, and destroy democracy*. New Press.

Nightingale, D. and Cromby, J. (eds) (1999) *Social Constructionist Psychology*. Buckingham: Open University Press.

Nygren, G. (2011) 'Passing Through Journalism? Journalism as a Temporary Job and Professional Institutions in Decline', in Franklin, B. and Mensing, D. (eds) *Journalism Education, Training and Employment*. London: Routledge.

Ognianova, E. and Endersby, J. (1996) 'Objectivity Revisited: A Spatial Model of Political Ideology and Mass Communication', *Journalism and Mass Communication Monographs* 159.

Örnebring, H. (2008a) The Two Professionalisms of Journalism: Updating Journalism Research for the 21st Century. Paper presented at the ICA conference, May 2008, in Toronto.

Örnebring, H. (2008b) 'The Producer as Consumer – of What? User-Generated Tabloid Content in The Sun (UK) and Aftonbladet (Sweden)', *Journalism Studies* 9(5) October: 771–785.

Oxford English Dictionary. (1997) Additions Series. Oxford: Oxford University Press.

Pavlik, J., Morgan, G. and Henderson, B. (2001) Information Technology: Implications for the Future of Journalism and Mass Communication Education. Report of the AEJMC Task Force on Teaching and Learning in the New Millenium (consulted May 2001), http://www.aejmc.org/pubs/2001.html.

Penn, W. Y. and Collier, B. D. (1985) 'Current Research in Moral Development as a Decision Support System', *Journal of Business Ethics* 4(2): 131–136.

Philo, G. (1982) *Really Bad News* (Vol. 3). Glasgow: Writers & Readers Publishing.

Pulitzer, J. (1904) 'Planning a School of Journalism', *North American Review*, http://centennial.journalism.columbia.edu/reflections/planning-a-school-of-journalism-the-basic-concept-in-1904-archival/.

Purkey, W. W. (1970) *Self-Concept and School Achievement*. New York: Prentice Hall.

Reese, S. (1990) 'The News Paradigm and the Ideology of Objectivity: A Socialist at the Wall Street Journal', *Critical Studies in Mass Communication* 7(4): 390–409.

Reese, S. (1999) 'Progressive Potential of Journalism Education: Recasting the Academic vs. Professional Debate', *Harvard International Journal of Press/Politics* 4(4): 70–94.

Reese, S. D. and Cohen, J. (2000) 'Educating for Journalism: The Professionalism of Scholarship', *Journalism Studies* 1(2): 213–227.

Rushkoff, D. (2003) *Open Source Democracy: How Online Communication Is Changing Offline Politics*, London: Demos, http://www.demos.co.uk/opensource democracy_pdf_media_public.aspx.

Russo, T. C. (1998) 'Organizational and Professional Identification: A Case of News- paper Journalists', *Management Communication Quarterly* 12(1): 72–111.

Sandelowski, M. and Barroso. J. (2002) 'Reading Qualitative Studies', *International Journal of Qualitative Methods* 1(1): Article 5, http://www.ualberta.ca/~ijqm/.

Schelsky, H. (1975) *Die Arbeit tun die anderen*. Opladen: Westdeuthcer Verlag.

Schudson, M. (1978) *Discovering the News*. New York: Basic Books.

Schudson, M. (2001) 'The Objectivity Norm in American Journalism', *Journalism* 2(2): 149–170.

Schudson, M. (2005) 'Four Approaches to the Sociology of News', in Curran, J. and Gurevitch. M. (eds) *Mass Media and Society*. London: Hodder Arnold, pp. 198–214.

Schlesinger, P. (1978) *Putting 'Reality' Together*. London: Methuen.

Selander, S. (1989) *Kampen om yrkesutovning, status och kunskap, professionaliseringens sociala grund [The Struggle About Occupations, Status and Knowledge, the Social Basis for Professionalisation]*. Lund: Studentlitteratur.

Shirky, C. (2000) 'RIP the Consumer, 1900–1999', *Clay Shirky's Writings about the Internet: Eco-nomics and Culture, Media and Community*, http://www.shirky.com/writings/consumer.html (accessed August 13, 2013).

Sigelman, L. (1973) 'Reporting the News: An Organisational Analysis', *American Journal of Sociology* 48: 132–151.

Singer, J. (1998) 'Online Journalists: Foundation for Research into Their Changing Roles', *Journal of Computer-Mediated Communication* 4(1), http://jcmc.huji.ac.il/vol4/issue1/singer.html.

Singer, J. (2003) 'Who Are These Guys? The Online Challenge to the Notion of Journalistic Professionalism', *Journalism* 4(2) May: 139–163.

Singer, J. (2004) 'Strange Bedfellows? The diffusion of convergence in four news organizations', *Journalism Studies* 5(1), pp. 3–18.

Skillset (2008) 'Journalism Skills Survey', http://www.creativeskillset.org/uploads/pdf/asset_13022.pdf?2 (accessed August 13, 2013).

Smircich, L. (1983) 'Concepts of Culture and Organizational Analysis', *Administrative Science Quarterly* 28(3): 339–358.

Snow, J. (2004) *Shooting History: A Personal Journey*, London: Harper Perennial.

Solomon, D. N. (1970) 'Role and Self Conception: Adaptation and Change in Occupations', in Shibutani, T. (ed.) *Human Nature and Collective Behaviour: Papers in Honor of Herbert Blumer*. Englewood Cliffs, NJ: Prentice Hall, pp. 286–300.

Soloski, J. (1990) 'News Reporting and Professionalism: Some Constraints on the Reporting of News', *Media, Culture and Society* 11(2): 207–228.

Stevens, J. (2002) 'TBO.com: Faces of Convergence'. *Online Journalism Review*, http://www.ojr.org/ojr/workplace/1017858783.php (accessed August 13, 2013).

Stevenson, N. (1995) *Understanding Media Cultures: Social Theory and Mass Communication*. London: Sage.

Sutton Trust (2006) *The educational backgrounds of leading journalists*. UK: The Sutton Trust.

Sutton Trust (2009) *The Educational Backgrounds of Leading Lawyers, Journalists, Vice Chancellors, Politicians, Medics and Chief Executives: The Sutton Trust Submission to the Milburn Commission on Access to the Professions*. UK: The Sutton Trust.

Taylor, C. (1985) *Human Agency and Language*. Cambridge: Cambridge University Press.

Teoh Kheng Yau, J. and Al-Hawamdeh, S. (2001) 'The Impact of the Internet on Teaching and Practicing Journalism', *Journal of Electronic Publishing* 7(1) (consulted September 2001), http://www.press.umich.edu/jep/07–01/al-hawamdeh.html.

Tickle, L. (2000) *Teacher Induction: The Way Ahead*. Buckingham, Philadelphia, PA: Open University Press.

Thomas, H. (2005, 13 April) Who You Calling a Journalist? Retrieved 19 July 2006, from http://www.channeloklahoma.com/helenthomas/4377193/detail.html.

Thurman, N. (2008) 'Forums for Citizen Journalists? Adoption of User Generated Content Initiatives by Online News Media', *New Media & Society*, 10(1), 139–157.

Trevino, L. K. (1992) 'Moral reasoning and business ethics: Implications for research, education, and management'. *Journal of Business Ethics*, 11(5–6), 445–459.

Tuchman, G. (1972) 'Objectivity as a Strategic Ritual: An Examination of Newsmen's Notions of Objectivity', *American Journal of Sociology*, 77: 660–679.

Tuchman, G. (1973) 'Making News by Doing Work: Routinizing the Unexpected', *American Journal of Sociology*, 78 (July, 1973): 110–131.

Tuchman, G. (1978) 'Professionalism as an agent of legitimation'. *Journal of Communication*, 28(2), 106–113.

Tuchman, G. (2003) 'The Production of News', in Klaus, B. J. (ed.) *A Handbook of Media and Communication Research: Qualitative and Quantitative Methodologies*. London: Routledge, pp. 78–90.

Tumber, H. and Palmer, J. (2004) *Media at War: The Iraq Crisis.* London: Sage.

Tumber, H. and Prentoulis, M. (2005) 'Journalism and the Making of a Profession', in de Burgh, H. (ed.) *Making Journalists: Diverse Models, Global Issues.* London and New York: Routledge, pp. 58–73.

Tumber, H. and Webster, F. (2006) *Journalists Under Fire: Information War and Journalistic Practices.* London: Sage.

Tunstall, J. (1971) *Journalists at Work.* London: Constable.

Tunstall, J. (1973) 'Journalism as an Occupation', *The Medico-Legal Journal* (Part Three): 87–101.

Ursell, G. (2003) 'Creating Value and Valuing Creativity in Contemporary UK Television: Or "Dumbing Down" the Workforce', *Journalism Studies* 4(1): 31–46.

van Ginneken, J. (1997) *Understanding Global News: A Critical Introduction.* London: Sage.

van Zoonen, L. (1998) 'A Professional, Unreliable, Heroic Marionette (M/F Structure, Agency and Subjectivity in Contemporary Journalisms', *European Journal of Cultural Studies* 1(1): 123–143.

Weaver, D. H. (2005) 'Who Are the Journalists? in Be Burgh, H. (ed.) *Making Journalists.* London and New York: Routledge, pp. 44–57.

Weaver, D. H., and Wilhoit., G. C. (1986) *The American Journalist: A Portrait of U.S. News People and Their Work.* Bloomington, IN: Indiana University Press.

Weber, M. (1973) 'Max Weber on Church, Sect and Mysticism', *Sociological Analysis* 34(2): 140–149.

Wheal, Chris (2005) *Regulating Journalists: A Consultation Document* (NUJ Professional Training Committee, http://www.docstoc.com/docs/17797622/Is-journalism-a-trade-or-a-profession (accessed February 2, 2013)).

White, D. M. (1950) 'The 'Gate Keeper': A Case Study in the Selection of News', *Journalism Quarterly* 27: 383–391.

Wise, R. (2000) *Multimedia: An Introduction.* London: Routledge.

Zelizer, B. (2004a) 'When Facts, Truth and Reality are God-terms: On Journalism's Uneasy Place in Cultural Studies', *Communication and Critical/Cultural Studies* 1(1): 100–119.

Zelizer, B. (2004b) *Taking Journalism Seriously: News and the Academy.* London: Sage.

Index

Note: Locators with letter 'n' refer to notes.